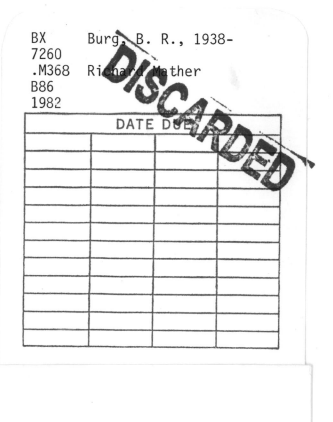

Richard Mather

Twayne's United States Authors Series

Mason Lowance, Editor

University of Massachusetts, Amherst

TUSAS 429

RICHARD MATHER
(1596-1669)
Courtesy of the American Antiquarian Society

Richard Mather

By B.R. Burg

Arizona State University

Twayne Publishers • *Boston*

Richard Mather

B.R. Burg

Copyright © 1982 by G.K. Hall & Company
Published by Twayne Publishers
A Division of G.K. Hall & Company
70 Lincoln Street
Boston, Massachusetts 02111

Book production by John Amburg
Book design by Barbara Anderson

Printed on permanent/durable acid-free
paper and bound in The United States of
America.

Library of Congress Cataloging in Publication Data

Burg, B. R. (Barry Richard), 1938–
Richard Mather.

(Twayne's United States authors series; TUSAS 429)
Bibliography: p. 132
Includes index.
1. Mather, Richard, 1596-1669. 2. Theology, Doctrinal—
New England—History—17th century. I. Title.
II. Series.
BX7260.M368B86   285.8'32'0924   82-932
ISBN 0-8057-7364-9   AACR2

For Jenny and John:
Two of the most recent migrants
to the eastern shore of North America

Contents

About the Author

B.R. Burg is Professor of History and Director of the College of Liberal Arts Honors Program at Arizona State University. He received the B.A. in Anthropology from the University of Colorado, the M.A. in Social Studies from Western State College, and the Ph.D. in History from the University of Colorado. He has served as a Ford Foundation Fellow with The Adams Papers and has been the recipient of a Shell Oil Company Foundation research grant, as well as numerous other awards. He is the author of a biography of Richard Mather, several fiction pieces, and has published scholarly articles in *The William and Mary Quarterly, Church History, American Neptune, Manuscripts,* and elsewhere. His book, *Sodomy and the Perception of Evil: English Sea Rovers in the Seventeenth-Century Caribbean,* will be published by New York University Press in 1982.

Preface

In the final months of the seventeenth century Cotton Mather, accomplished scholar, minister to the city of Boston's North Church, and eminent Protestant divine, set out to chronicle the ecclesiastical history of New England from the first settlement at Plymouth in 1620 until the year 1698. "I write the Wonders of the Christian Religion, flying from the Depravations of Europe to the American Strand," he said in his introduction, and throughout the seven volumes that followed he integrated God's Providence with the history, literature, and life of the colonies he memorialized. The first several pages of Mather's *Magnalia Christi Americana* are a joyous celebration of Christ's triumphs in the New World, and no writer in America until the time of Walt Whitman equaled Mather's uninhibited enthusiasm in describing the glories of his land. Yet while the shepherd of the North Church declaimed eloquently and at length in commemoration of what had been achieved, the tone and direction of his efforts contrasted sharply with the work of a previous generation of colonial clerics. In earlier decades the founders of New England's faith wasted little ink on the wonders of America. They struggled instead to build a viable community amid a fearful wilderness and to establish God's word on an alien shore some thousands of miles from established Christian society.

Cotton Mather's grandfather, the Reverend Richard Mather, was one of the many clergymen who came to the Massachusetts Bay Colony during its early years of settlement, and like most of the first generation of colonial clerics, when he wrote he did not waste time giving grandeur to what had been accomplished. He wrote to strengthen Christ's churches and to defend and preserve them for posterity. The works that came from his pen were technical treatises, descriptions of religious practice, discussions of ecclesiastical controversies, justification for interpretations of Scripture, and exhortations to follow biblical commandment. Nowhere in his writings, even in his few surviving letters, is there tenderness and devotion like that which John Winthrop expressed in his notes to his wife, nor is there in his treatises the same sense of awe and humility found in the work of William Bradford. Mather's writings are emphatically purposeful, conceived and promulgated for the accomplishment of specified theological tasks. He seldom drifted from pursuit of his goals or engaged in lengthy digression, and only rarely did he inject himself into his work.

The lack of sensitivity or ardor in his major treatises has led to the assumption, even among those who had read him carefully, that Mather's failure to communicate subjective understanding of his emotions or to project his prodigious vitality to modern readers indicates that he faced similar difficulties with his seventeenth-century readership. It is very unlikely that this was the case, but such criticisms of Mather's work, even if justified, relate only to the political ramifications of his efforts. His most profound and lasting contribution, far outweighing his influence in minor ecclesiastical squabbles, was the effect his literary techniques and ideological innovation had on the maturation of American literature and thought in the seventeenth and eighteenth centuries. This is not apparent in his earlier works, those written in England and during his first ten years in the Massachusetts Bay Colony, but by the 1640s Mather had learned his craft and become sufficiently confident of his acceptance into the settlement's ministerial brotherhood so that he could venture beyond the constrictions that limited him in earlier years. It was only then that he infused his works with a new element of force and struck out first against the colony's detractors and then against its government. Later, when Mather remained the only living representative of Massachusetts Bay's first generation of ministers, his writing often lamented the spiritual decay he perceived in the colony, but even here he was not overtaken by the maudlin sentimentality that often becomes the essence of the works of aged men. His exhortations were weighted with the burden of his years, but his theology remained crisp, incisive, and as purposeful as the letters and treatises he wrote during his first decade in America.

Still, the general direction of Mather's work over forty years is less important than the questions raised by the technical innovation and ideological expansion of his writing and preaching from the time of his earliest surviving piece in 1635 to his final defenses of extended baptism after 1662. The problem in this respect is, in part, to analyze the changes and alterations Mather brought to the colony's ecclesiastical writing, pulpit oratory, and theology, but of equal importance is the need to evaluate the impact of his work on clerics who came after him, the men who adopted his methods and sentiments and made them a part of American ecclesiastical thought and practice by the close of the seventeenth century, through the Great Awakening, and on into the era of the Revolution. The primary object of this study, then, is not only to ascertain the effect of Mather's work on the redirection of New England writing and preaching but to analyze the foundations he laid for techniques that would become commonplace in later decades.

Although Mather wrote both poetry and prose, his surviving verses are few in number and treat subjects so far removed from those dealt with in his prose that they have no value to this study. The most effective method of illustrating Mather's ideology and technique is to use quotations from his treatises, polemics, and sermons. Sometimes passages are used alone to substantiate a point, at other times selections from two or more of his works are compared to demonstrate vacillations or maturation, and occasionally portions of his work are compared with those of his colleagues to integrate his writings with the works of other Bay Colony authors.

The first chapter is concerned largely with religious and political events in England in the sixteenth and early seventeenth centuries since it was against the organization and operation of his nation's secular and ecclesiastical order that Mather reacted. His first surviving writings deal with problems created by the policies of Charles I and his churchmen, and without an understanding of English events in these years, Mather's earliest work would have no meaning. A discussion of institutions in the Massachusetts Bay Colony, particularly the local churches, is included in Chapter 2, not only to provide information on the type of church order that dictated the form of Mather's first writings in America, but because some knowledge of Bay Colony doctrine, theology, and ecclesiastical organization is essential to an understanding of all Mather's writings for the final three decades of his life.

Chapter 3 explores the motives and methods behind what were to become Mather's most widely known works, *Church Government . . . an Answer to Two and Thirty Questions* and *An Apologie for Church Covenant.* Both treatises were produced to accomplish the necessary tasks of insuring conformity in Massachusetts Bay's religion during the first years of settlement when the colonists were laboring to build churches in accordance with God's command while at the same time thousands of migrants poured in, many of whom did not share the original colonists' perceptions of the nature of reformed Christianity. Mather's sermons, or those of them that survive, are the subject of the fourth chapter, and in the tightly structured arguments he presented week after week and month after month in the Dorchester meeting-house, one can see not only the manner in which Mather structured his sermons, but also gain glimpses of the theological innovator who unobtrusively restructured puritan-style theology to fit the needs of his parishioners in a tiny New England village. This is done by examining a surviving set of Mather's sermons in which he attempted to draw out God's plan for salvation and explain it to his congregants in a way that would quiet many of their spiritual anxieties and encourage them to believe that they were closer to God than they normally would have imagined. Chapter 5 deals with the reforms Mather introduced into the colony's church-state relationship, detailing how he first proposed serious modifications in his draft of church government presented to the synod of 1648, exploring some of the justifications he used to convince his colleagues of the wisdom of such changes, and describing the nature of the alterations in church-state relations adopted as the result of his efforts.

The next chapter examines Mather's writings on intrachurch administration and on the need to extend eligibility for baptism to previously unbaptized members of the Massachusetts Bay community. Most of the work discussed in the chapter was written in Mather's last years, the period between 1662 and his death in 1669. The conclusion surveys the effect of Richard Mather's work and presents an evaluation of his influence on preaching and writing in early America.

Over the past fifty years those who have studied the first settlers of the Bay Colony have worked successfully to broaden understanding of the early English migrants to America. Almost all have accepted the dictum that human beings are far too important to be regarded only as symptoms of the past. In their books and articles they have not only turned John Winthrop, Roger Williams, John Cotton, and Increase Mather from historical silhouettes into full-bodied human beings, but they have examined and analyzed the writings of these men, their journals, diaries, sermons, treatises, and tracts, seeking always to discover more about the beginnings of the doctrine and ideology that became the base for American intellectual evolution. Over the past three hundred years no one has attempted to examine the work of Richard Mather with the same care that has been expended on the labors of other Bay Colony clerics. Although several who knew him in England and America wrote accounts of his life, none of the biographers saw fit to compose analytic assessments of his career. The men who wrote of him were too closely allied by ideological or consanguinary bonds to be concerned with the details of his work. Instead, like those who chronicled his life in the nineteenth century, they sought to polish his image, to make him larger than life, and in some cases to use his theological judgments for their own purposes.

The result of three centuries of highly partisan and unevenly constructed analysis is a Richard Mather who emerges from the past only as a shadow. But even more important, since Mather's writings have been largely ignored, it raises the question of why a man of his talent and ability has never been recognized for his accomplishments but instead is most widely known only as the father of Increase Mather and the grandfather of Cotton Mather.

The cause of Mather's obscurity is not particularly difficult to discover. Much of his work was written for local consumption and circulated only in manuscript form among the colony's clergymen. In contrast, a substantial portion of the writings by men recognized as leading Massachusetts Bay clerics was composed to influence nonconformists in England as well as in America, and their manuscripts were sent to London, printed, and disseminated widely in England, Scotland, Ireland, and ultimately in New England. The large editions and wide distribution of works, especially those by John Cotton, meant that over the years their books, pamphlets, and miscellaneous writings were easily available to scholars, writers, and historians of early American literature. At the same time much of Mather's work remained in manuscript, not because it was deficient in quality but because it was written to be read by only a few more than three score clerics who lived in nearby New England villages. With colonial printing facilities expensive and strictly limited, the most convenient way to circulate ideas cheaply and with expedition was to make several copies of each work and pass them out among those to be influenced. Most of these manuscripts later found their way into print, but the editions were usually small, distribution was restricted, and like Mather's manuscripts, his published works were not as easily available to investigators as were the writings of others.

In modern America it is difficult to conceive of anyone affecting the course of a substantive ideological disagreement by having his arguments passed from man to man in handwritten form, but it must not be forgotten that when Mather wrote over three hundred years ago the process of manual distribution was a widely practiced and generally accepted method of diffusing ideas. It should be remembered, too, that Mather and his ministerial colleagues were the intellectual offspring of men whose writings were condemned in England and could not be legally printed. During the reigns of Elizabeth and James I, with licenses to publish denied them, Protestant religious dissenters, or nonconformists as they were often called, maintained an underground communications network for promulgating their thoughts on ecclesiastical matters. They did this by copying and recopying their sermons, tracts, and polemics, and sending them out among members of their clerical brotherhood where, in chain-letter fashion, more copies were made and the distribution continued. When in England, Richard Mather and his associates formed a part of this network, and the habits of the past did not disappear simply because they traversed the Atlantic. The hand-copied manuscripts passed from cleric to cleric remained the most common means for communicating ecclesiastical ideology in Massachusetts Bay until the need to reach a wider audience was recognized after the synod of 1662.

Although seventeenth-century writers used a profusion of abbreviations for proper names, conjunctions, prefixes, and suffixes, none of these have been retained in the quotations used in this study. The capitalization, punctuation, and inconsistent orthography of three hundred years ago have been modernized when necessary, but the modifications have been kept to a minimum to preserve as much as possible of the original meaning and direction of the writings. Words that cannot be deciphered because of crabbed handwriting, smears, or damage to manuscript materials are noted by the abbreviation "illeg." bracketed at the place within the quotations where they appear. Lengthy seventeenth-century book and pamphlet titles are shortened in the text, notes, and in the bibliography.

Because of the limitations of space, the many who aided me in my work on Richard Mather cannot be thanked individually, but a few organizations and persons must be acknowledged by name because of their extraordinary efforts on my behalf. I am especially indebted to the Faculty Grants Committee of Arizona State University for funding a portion of my research. The University Press of Kentucky was particularly kind in allowing me to use previously published material on Mather for this study. I would also like to thank Paul Hubbard of Arizona State University and Clifford L. Egan of the University of Houston, both of whom said kind words about me when they were especially needed. An additional measure of gratitude is owed to Ms. Beth Luey who provided me with trenchant observations on Richard Mather's character.

B. R. Burg

Arizona State University

Chronology

1596   Richard Mather born in Lowtown, a village near Liverpool, the son of Margrett and Thomas Mather.

1602   Enrolled at the free grammar school in Winwick, probably between 1602 and 1604.

1611   Leaves his studies at Winwick to teach Latin and Greek at a newly opened grammar school in nearby Toxteth Park.

1614   Undergoes a profound religious conversion that convinces him he has been chosen by God for salvation.

1618   Leaves Toxteth Park and begins studies at Brasenose College, Oxford. After spending only six months at the University he returns to Toxteth Park, not as schoolmaster but as the village minister.

1619   Ordained as a cleric in the Church of England by Thomas Morton, the Bishop of Chester.

1624   Marries Katharine Hoult, the daughter of Squire Edmund Hoult of nearby Bury.

1630   Selected to deliver part of a series of sermons to stem the growth of Roman Catholicism in Liverpool.

1633   Removed from his pulpit for nonconformity, reinstated, then removed permanently in late November or early December.

1635   Writes "The Removing from Old England to New." Migrates to the Massachusetts Bay Colony. Admitted to the First Church in Boston after writing "Some Objections Against Imposition in Ordination" to convince the church elders and members he understands the ordination ceremony.

1636   Moves to Dorchester to organize a church in March, but the church is not given official approval by the General Court until August.

1637   Translates several of the Psalms from Hebrew into English for inclusion in *The Bay Psalm Book.*

1639   Writes two justifications of the Massachusetts Bay Colony's religious practices in answer to inquiries from nonconforming clerics in England. A sixth son, Increase, is born to the Mathers.

1643   The two justifications of colonial religion published in London as *An Apologie* and *Church Government . . . an Answer to Two and Thirty Questions.*

1643   General Court requests Mather to deliver the annual election sermon.

1644   With clerical colleague William Tompson he writes *A Modest and Brotherly Answer to Mr. Charles Herle* in reply to Herle's attack on Bay Colony church government. Writes his *Reply to Mr. Rutherford* in response to portions of Samuel Rutherford's *Due Right of Presbyteries.*

1646   Completes "A Plea for the Churches of Christ in New England" and his attack on the work of John Spilsbury. Ordered by the synod to prepare a statement of church discipline for the Bay Colony. Begins preaching the series of sermons that will later be collected and entitled "The Summe of Seventie Lectures."

1648   Presents his "Modell of Church-Government" to the meeting of the synod.

1649   His draft platform of church government is modified, endorsed by the synod, and published as *The Cambridge Platform.*

1650   With William Tompson, publishes *An Heart-Melting Exhortation* begging friends and parishioners left behind in Lancashire to repent or be destroyed. Also publishes two catechisms, one for adults, the other for children.

1652   Publishes *The Summe of Certain Sermons upon Genes: 15. 6.*

1657   Meeting of Bay Colony clerics endorses broadening eligibility for baptism. Mather compiles a record of their deliberations later published as *A Disputation Concerning Church Members and Their Children*. Also publishes *A Farewel-Exhortation to the Church and People of Dorchester*.

1662   Participates in the synod that gives formal approval to the half-way covenant.

1664   Engages in polemical battle with opponents of the synod's decisions. Publishes *A Defense of the Answer and Arguments of the Synod Met at Boston in the Year 1662*.

1669   Appointed moderator of assembly convened to settle disagreements within the First Church in Boston. Dies in April.

1670   His son Increase Mather publishes *The Life and Death of That Reverend Man of God, Mr. Richard Mather*.

1712   Mather's *An Answer to Two Questions: Whether Does the Power of Church Government Belong to All the People or to the Elders Alone* published posthumously.

Chapter One
The World of Richard Mather: England under the Early Stuarts

The seventeenth century was a tumultuous time in England. It was an age of bloody civil war and wrenching social disruption, a time when an older order was destroyed and none could be found to take its place. It was an era when men proclaimed the divine right of kings as they passed a sentence of death on their sovereign, and clerics preached that God commanded only one church while sects and denominations proliferated. Yet an England torn by strife and faction was not the sort of land into which Richard Mather was born on a forgotten day in 1596. By the time of his birth, the nation had been a peaceful place for over one hundred years. Stability had returned to England after the end of the Wars of the Roses in 1485, and although there had been severe religious disruptions in the land throughout the first half of the sixteenth century, these seemed to be a part of the past. The difficulties that remained in the closing decade of the century hardly appeared serious enough to threaten the nation. Some argued that Spain had to be watched carefully, but the defeat of the Spanish Armada in 1588 meant that there was no prospect England would be overwhelmed. Others worried over the claims of Mary Stuart to the throne, but their fears evaporated when she fell victim to the headsman's axe. There had been some concern over corruption in the national church, but those who complained on this account were few in number, and since the elevation of John Whitgift to the Archbishopric of Canterbury it was difficult to consider them dangerous.

Mathers had lived in Lancashire over one hundred years by the time the Armada was destroyed, but though the name, spelled Madur, Madowr, and with several other variations, is found in every sort of local record, little is known of individual members of the family. An

entry in the parish register for the village of Warrington is typical of
the meagerness of the surviving evidence. Dated September 30, 1591,
and inscribed in a hand somewhat larger than the items that precede
it and those that follow, it reads, "Thomas Mather and Margrett
Abra[ms] the same."[1] This brief record of a marriage is almost the
only remaining trace of the couple who became the parents of Richard
Mather. Richard was born only a short distance from Liverpool, in the
tiny hamlet of Lowtown, but beyond the place and year of birth, little
is known of his early life. He was probably raised amid a welter of
brothers, sisters, cousins, uncles, and aunts, for the Mather women
produced scores of children in every generation, but despite the
profusion of Lancashire Mathers, it is likely that no member of the
family had prospered sufficiently by the end of the sixteenth century to
have become a member of the squirearchy. Though the family was of
ordinary stock, Richard's father was not one of the many landless
agricultural laborers or unskilled workers found in the villages
scattered about the countryside. He appears to have been a speculator
or a member of the growing and acquisitive class of artisans, traders,
and shopkeepers that abounded in Tudor England.

Like many young men of his middling social rank, Richard Mather
was given the opportunity to acquire basic academic skills. The first
surviving evidence of his youthful concerns dates from the time he
began his scholarly training, though the record is only in the form of
a recollection. Years later in New England he once told his youngest
son that he never truly understood why his parents had chosen to send
him to school rather than apprentice him to an artisan or tradesman.

Mather's earliest experiences as a student were exceedingly unpleas-
ant, for the master was harsh on his young charges and continual
application of the rod was extremely discouraging. At one point the
beginning scholar from Lowtown asked his parents to terminate his
education, but the elder Mather refused. Instead, he told his son he
would speak with the master and ask him to be less severe in his
application of punishment. Richard did not record whether his father
kept the promise or if the instructor was willing to accede to the
parental request, but he did continue his education. His only comment
on the conclusion of the episode was the wistfully expressed hope "that
all Schoolmasters would learn Wisdome, Moderation and Equity

towards their Scholars, and seek rather to win the hearts of Children by righteous, loving, and courteous usage, than to alienate their mindes by partiality and undue severity, which had been my utter undoing, had not the good Providence of God, and the Wisdome and Authority of my Father prevented.''[2]

Richard was an able student in his grammar school years, although none of his actions indicated any abiding concern for spiritual matters. He was exposed to Christian doctrine and theology on a regular basis, as were all Englishmen in the seventeenth century, but the sermons of the preacher at nearby Legh, where he attended church, and the inculcation of Holy Writ at school did not induce in him any intense religious feeling. The young man's casual approach to religion was shared by members of his immediate family. The lack of spiritual commitment in the household was particularly apparent when Thomas Mather went through a period of financial distress when Richard was in his early teens. At that time several Catholic merchants were passing through Warrington looking for youngsters to be apprenticed to them. The elder Mather, though the head of a Protestant household, feared he could no longer afford the supplementary expense required for his son's education at the free school. He decided to bind him to the tradesmen, and it was only a last-minute intercession on the part of the local schoolmaster that changed his mind and enabled the youthful scholar to continue his academic career.[3]

Though the Mathers were not greatly concerned with ecclesiastical matters, they were undoubtedly aware of the basic theological disagreements that divided the country in the first years of the seventeenth century. The specific religious issues separating Englishmen were varied and complex, but one of the most serious was the question of Roman Catholic influence remaining in the national church. When Henry VIII broke with Rome, he was content to keep English religion much as it was before the split. The only structural changes he effected were the substitution of himself in place of the Pope as head of the church and the dissolution of the monasteries. Henry's rejection of the Catholic church did not mean that he was willing to accept the beliefs of Continental reformers who sought to restructure Christianity completely. Worship in England continued to include confession, transubstantiation, clerical celibacy, prayers for the dead, and observance of monastic vows. Severe penalties were decreed for denying officially established beliefs, and a number of ecclesiastical dignitaries, including Sir Thomas More, were executed for their refusal to pay the required deference to the royal determinations on matters of faith.

When Henry died, he was succeeded on the throne by Edward VI, the son of his marriage to Jane Seymour. The new king was only nine years old at the time of his accession, and a regency headed by his uncle, the Duke of Somerset, actually governed in his name. Somerset proved to be an inept leader, and he was removed from his position by the Duke of Northumberland and several of the regents. Northumberland was an energetic champion of the Protestant cause, and under his direction, great efforts were made to free English religion of all vestiges of its Catholic past. Upon the death of Edward VI, after a reign of only six years, Northumberland attempted to perpetuate his Protestant regime by naming as queen Lady Jane Grey, a grandniece of Henry VIII, but his religious policies had generated considerable hostility and there was widespread fear of Northumberland himself. He was deserted by many of his supporters who then gave their loyalty to Henry's daughter, Mary Tudor. She became queen in 1553.

Queen Mary, a child of Henry's marriage to Catharine of Aragon, was raised as a Catholic, and her religious training convinced her that she was chosen by God to restore England to the Roman fold. At first Mary's attempts to reverse the course of the nation's faith were successful. Parliament repealed all laws touching on religion that were passed during Edward's reign and they formally welcomed a Papal legate who forgave England and admitted the country back into the Church of Rome. The Queen then proceded to undo much of the regency's work, and many who refused to accept her counterreformation were intimidated, forced into exile, or even burned at the stake. The extent and excessive cruelty of the persecutions visited on those who opposed her religious policies alienated much of Mary's support, and the subsequent decline in her popularity, when combined with unfavorable economic conditions in England and the steady growth of Protestantism in Scotland, undermined her fragile health. After ruling only five years, Mary died in 1558.

Princess Elizabeth, the daughter of the union of Henry VIII and Anne Boleyn, succeeded Mary as queen, and since the marriage of her parents had been condemned by the Papacy, she was necessarily a Protestant. Although Elizabeth was not a deeply religious woman, she realized that some kind of religious settlement was vital to bring stability to England. The efforts to purge the nation's religion of Roman practice, suspended since the days of Edward VI, were revived, and Parliament responded to the new situation by passing the Act of Supremacy in 1559 requiring Elizabeth to be recognized as "Supreme Governor" of the Church of England. Further laws were enacted compelling Englishmen to worship in the fashion instituted under Edward VI, and Mary's Catholic bishops were removed from office and their places filled by Protestants. Later, in a final act of religious settlement, Thirty-nine Articles of Faith were adopted in which the phraseology and doctrine were purposely vague so that a broad base of support could be had for the national church.

The intensity of the reaction to Mary's ecclesiastical policies was augmented by the return of many extreme Protestants who had fled England between 1553 and 1558. While in exile they had imbibed the spirit of Frankfort, Geneva, and other Continental centers of the Reformation, and on their return they were determined to model England's religion after these European examples. They demanded that the Church eliminate all elements of doctrine and ceremony not specifically sanctioned by the Bible. They insisted on simplicity in worship and the abolition of every useless relic from the pre-Reformation past. The reformers hoped to replace the Mass with sermons, they raged against all sacraments except baptism and communion, most demanded the removal from the churches of altars, communion rails, statuary, and the stations of the cross. All insisted on the use of English rather than Latin, and they complained of the nonbiblical origins of a multitude of doctrinal and ceremonial procedures. Some of the more extreme reformers, while sharing all the dissatisfactions of their more moderate associates, insisted that reform must go further than simply a superficial cleansing. They demanded the elimination of the episcopal system of ecclesiastical government which placed control of the churches in the hands of a hierarchy of archbishops, bishops, and lesser officials.

The returned exiles were not the only Englishmen who favored reform of the Church of England in the years after 1558. There were large numbers in the land who were also dissatisfied with the national religion, but among them was wide divergence of opinion on the manner and extent to which it should be changed. Some nonconformists wanted only moderate ceremonial alteration but others demanded a sweeping reconstitution of the Church. Under Elizabeth, acceptable compromises were reached on most religious matters, and although the Roman style of church government was retained, the theology of the national church was brought more in line with the demands of Protestantism. The modifications that were made diminished the power of those who demanded even more sweeping reforms, and the queen's consummate political skill kept the extremists from becoming a serious problem.

It was not until the throne passed to James I, in 1603, that the reformers again thought they had cause for optimism. Their new king was a Scotsman, and presumably sympathetic with the Scottish church where all ceremonies and doctrines that smacked of Rome were rigorously suppressed. Even before he arrived in London to receive his crown, reformers presented him with the Millenary Petition, a request for wide-ranging ecclesiastical reform signed by approximately a thousand clerics, and later at a conference at Hampton Court in 1604 James heard an assembly of nonconformists request a simplification of ceremonies and the elimination of a series of abuses from the Church of England. Unfortunately for the reformers, their hopes were to be disappointed. It was soon apparent that James was more interested in preserving his temporal throne than in heeding the nonconformists' interpretation of God's word. He rejected the demands for purification, and while agreeing to authorize a new translation of the Bible and make several minor liturgical changes, he refused to lead England along a new ecclesiastical course. Instead he gave his full support to the Anglican establishment that had matured under Elizabeth.

One group of nonconformists, frustrated by the policies of their ruler and despairing of church reform, migrated to the Low Countries where they were free to observe God's commandments without interference from the authorities, but most who were disappointed at the failure of James I to sponsor more reformation did not choose this extreme course. They elected instead to remain in England and work for ecclesiastical reorganization even though they did so without the blessing of their sovereign.

Like his predecessor, James was able to contain the threat from those who sought to modify the church even though their ranks continued to grow and the volume of their denunciations increased. Lacking royal favor and distressed by a church that seemed to be moving away from their doctrines instead of toward them (at least on the higher levels of ecclesiastical officialdom), the nonconformists continued to work. Since they were unable to institute change by official decree, they labored to encourage the adoption of their reforms on the parish level. Extreme segments of nonconformity were particularly successful in this activity, and many clerics who originally objected only to minor Roman ceremonial practices were urged to defy the hierarchy and adopt a whole range of reforms in their local churches. Large numbers of ministers discarded their vestments, altered or refused to observe the requirements delineated in the *Book of Common Prayer,* and conducted their services with an emphasis on preaching rather than on what they came to consider hollow ritual. Nonconformist sentiment grew so powerful in some localities that many clerics managed to institute both reformed worship and church government in most of the parishes in their dioceses.

The king and his church did not entirely ignore the growth of dissent, and after 1620 those who refused to conform to established religious practice were persecuted. They were denied the right to hold some public offices, they were harassed by officials of the hierarchy, and some clerics were removed from their pulpits, but at no time was the persecution as vigorous, constant, or severe as it had been under Mary.

Nonconformity had grown strong in Lancashire during the first decade of the seventeenth century, but while reformed religion increased its sway in the country, young Richard Mather was probably more concerned with his own misfortunes than with the growth of theological dissent. In 1611 he was forced to conclude his studies when the people of Toxteth Park, a village some twenty miles from his birthplace, asked the master of his school to suggest a likely lad to instruct at the academy they had recently erected. Mather was recommended for the post, and although he had hoped to go on to a university, not to a thinly populated area like Toxteth Park, his father accepted the offer. The adolescent scholar, not yet sixteen years old, began his first employment as a teacher of Latin and Greek.[4]

Throughout his tenure as a schoolmaster, Mather lived with the Edward Aspinwalls of Toxteth Park, and he later wrote that the strongly nonconformist family exerted a continuous influence on him. Over the weeks and months he resided in their house, he gradually became concerned with the difference between his mode of life and that of his deeply religious hosts. He first experienced a prolonged uneasiness over his spiritual condition and this was followed by several periods of restlessness and worry. Mather's suffering was not an unusual experience for a young man to undergo in early seventeenth-century England, but he had read and heard of others who found they were among the elect only after passing through a time of supplication and prayer, and so he set a similar regimen for himself. In due course, his efforts were successful. Amid tears and cries of joy, he realized as he kneeled beside a Lancashire hedge on a day in 1614 that he was one of God's chosen.[5]

After he received assurance that he was a recipient of divine grace, a much more comfortable Mather continued as master of the Toxteth Park school. It was not until four years later that he left his classroom and entered Oxford to expand his religious and intellectual qualifications. His reasons for leaving the position as a schoolmaster to enroll at the university are not known, but his previous desire to attend and the suspension of his classes while a chapel was being built adjoining the school were probably responsible for the decision.

Richard Mather matriculated at Brasenose College, Oxford, in the spring of 1618. The young scholar was appreciative of the new liberty to engage in intellectual activity, and probably found the academic atmosphere a welcome relief from his duties as master at Toxteth Park. All was not perfect, however, and with the zeal of the newly saved, he complained loudly of his distress at the degree of profaneness and superstition he observed in many of the other students. Still, this was only a minor irritation when there was so much to be done. Prayers, Bible study, debates, lectures, and the writings of reformed clerics occupied the major portion of Mather's academic activities, and, as he read and studied, his commitment to nonconformity deepened while he fell more and more under the sway of several of Protestantism's foremost theologians.[6]

The usual length of time for a scholar to remain at Oxford and complete his studies was seven years, but Mather spent only a few months at Brasenose before he was asked by the people of Toxteth Park to return and serve as their minister. Other factors in addition to the request influenced his decision to leave the university and go back to the village, but the only clue to their nature is the brief phrase in a biography later written by his son stating, "After due Consideration, for weighty Reasons he accepted of."[7]

With his departure from Oxford, Richard Mather ended the period of his life wherein he labored as a scholar and schoolmaster and entered the ministry of the God he was to serve for the next fifty-one years.

By accepting the offer to become minister of Toxteth Park, Richard Mather naturally became a participant in the raging conflict between nonconformists and the established church, but in 1618 his difficulties with doctrinal deviation were still in the future. His first experiences as a cleric were pleasant enough, hardly reflecting the intense religious dissatisfaction that was dividing the English nation. When he returned, he found a new chapel ready for use. The man who preceded him departed before the building was complete, and the returned Oxonian became the first to mount the untried rostrum. He preached his maiden sermon on November 30, and, according to his son, Mather's initial attempt to do the work of the Lord was well received—at least by the judicious members of the congregation. Evidently the clerical version of stage fright accompanied the new pastor during the preparation of his first exhortation, for anxiety at the thought of finishing too soon caused him to prepare enough material for several sermons. Mather soon overcame his uneasiness in the pulpit, but even after he became used to preaching, he knew he could not conduct the religious affairs of the village indefinitely without ordination. The people of Toxteth Park urged him to take part in the ceremony that would officially confirm his position, and before a year was out he had agreed. As one of a group of candidates for the ministry, he was ordained by the Bishop of Chester.[8]

Mather, now a cleric in the Church of England, continued the work he began the previous year, serving his congregation at Toxteth Park. The young man's pastoral rounds were not confined to his own village, but extended into the surrounding countryside. He delivered two sermons each Lord's day for his own flock, preached once each fortnight on Wednesday at the neighboring town of Prescot, exhorted at other locations on holy days, and preached at funerals. As was the case when Mather was a schoolmaster, the duties of the occupation did not absorb all of his time. After his installation as minister of the chapel, he became the suitor of Katharine Hoult, the daughter of Edmund Hoult of Bury. "She had (and that deservedly) the repute of a very godly and prudent Maid," but her father objected to the union because he was not enthusiastic about gaining a nonconforming son-in-law. With encouragement from Miss Hoult, Mather persisted in his suit. It took several years before the squire could be persuaded to give his daughter's hand. Some clue to the father's change of heart might be found in an examination of the calendar. The two were married on September 29, 1624 and their first son, Samuel, was born only a scant seven and one half months later.[9] Two more children followed shortly thereafter: Timothy was born in 1628 and Nathaniel in 1630.[10]

By all evidence, Mather's ministry was successful during his first years of marriage. When the Lord Mayor of Liverpool and several members of the town corporation requested two sermons per month to stem the tide of Catholicism, he was one of those selected to deliver the series. To insure that the sermons reflected the doctrines of the Church of England accurately, the bishop ordered the appointed ministers to preach in a manner "conformeable to the Canons of the Church." By this time Mather was already a staunch nonconformist, but in Lancashire, where there was widespread deviation from the doctrine and ceremony of strictly prescribed Anglicanism, it easily passed unnoticed. Though informers were present at the services to discover "whether any preacher there speake or doe any thinge to prejudice the doctrine or discipline of the Church of England," his sermons, delivered in April and August of 1630, attracted no unfavorable attention from the authorities.[11]

Even though Mather's deviation from the faith and ceremonies demanded by the Archbishops of Canterbury and York was not extreme, it soon came into conflict with the rapidly changing religious climate in England. Charles I, having succeeded to the throne in 1625, was intent on demonstrating that he would not be as lenient in religious matters as James had been, and the hierarchy began to reflect these feelings. A cleric of high church principles, Richard Neile, was elevated to the Archbishopric of York in 1631, and shortly thereafter William Laud was placed in the See of Canterbury. Both men were determined to enforce rigid conformity to the canons of the Church of England.

In the general tightening of discipline that followed Neile's installation, Mather came to the notice of the authorities, and the Bishop of Chester, whose diocese included Toxteth Park, ordered him removed from his pulpit in 1633. Fortunately for the cleric, he was not without friends in these difficult moments. He was championed by a group of persons who wielded influence with several members of the hierarchy. By November they were able to gain his reinstatement and he returned to his flock. If Mather had nurtured the hope that his persecution was at an end when he returned to his pulpit at Toxteth Park, he was mistaken. His encounter with the diocese was over, but he had yet to deal with the Archbishop of York, and it was only a short time after he was restored to his church, in the autumn of 1633, that his nonconformity carried him again into difficulty. Operating under the jurisdiction of Archbishop Neile, a board of investigators arrived in the village of Wigan near Toxteth Park in late November or early December, 1633. Either because of his earlier record of suspension or as the result of new reports of nonconformity on his part, Mather was called before the conclave to answer for his religious conduct.[12] He was understandably distressed at being summoned before the board, but his previous experience with removal and reinstatement gave him cause not to fear the second attempt to silence him.

Some idea of the mood and temper of the court on that day surfaced in a brief exchange that took place when one of the inquisitors asked Mather how long he had been a cleric. He replied that he had been occupied at the task for some fifteen years. He was next asked about the length of time he had worn a surplice. His reply that he had never worn one had an incendiary effect on the interrogator, and he shouted to those present, "What . . . preach Fifteen years and never wear a Surpless? It had been better for him that he had gotten Seven Bastards." The investigators suspended Mather for the second time. If there were any more attempts to have him reinstated, they were ineffectual, and the suspension remained in force.[13]

Having been removed from his position as minister of the chapel at

Toxteth Park for the second time, and with almost no chance of being restored, Mather retired to private life after a decade and a half spent serving his rural congregation.

By this time the increasingly rigid enforcement of the discipline demanded by the Church of England had encouraged migration to the Massachusetts Bay Colony, and the subject of departure for the New World was discussed by many nonconforming clerics, including those in Lancashire. The Bay Colony's reputation as a refuge for persecuted nonconformists was greatly enhanced in 1633 when John Cotton joined the New Englanders. After his removal from St. Botolph's Church in Lincolnshire, Cotton had originally planned on traveling to the Low Countries, but a fortunate chain of circumstances instead carried him across the Atlantic with Thomas Hooker, another dissenting cleric. Mather was well aware of the advantages that could be gained by migration. After their arrival in the colony, both Cotton and Hooker wrote letters to their fellow nonconformists in England describing the wonders of Massachusetts Bay, and by the time of his most serious difficulties with the hierarchy, Mather had already acquired copies of the letters written by these two men.[14]

"The Removing from Old England to New"

Arguments advanced by Cotton and Hooker may have been sufficient to induce some to undertake the voyage to New England, but Mather was not close enough to abandoning his home so that the letters from migrants, even those with impressive nonconforming credentials, would precipitate his decision to cross the Atlantic.[15] He was a careful man, and before he could make a decision of such magnitude he first had to evaluate the question at great length, trying as best he could to discover the wisest course of action. In the weeks after he was dismissed from his pulpit, Mather wrote out a monologue to aid in assessing the relative strengths and weaknesses of the alternatives available to him. His work revealed that he relied heavily on the letters written to nonconforming clerics by Cotton and Hooker after their arrival in the Bay Colony. He read of Hooker's belief, expressed without a trace of equivocation, that there was no place on earth where men could do more spiritual good to themselves and others than in Massachusetts Bay, and he included the same reason in

"The Removing from Old England to New," his manuscript discussion of emigration. To journey "to a place where one may have well-grounded hope of preservation, and of God's protection, is necessary," he said, and then added, "Ministers being free, are bound to remove, if they be in such place where they may not govern their own Flocks."[16] Cotton's letter, addressed to "A Puritan Minister in England," and written to be circulated widely among dissenting clerics in the homeland also influenced Mather deeply. It was obvious, Cotton wrote, that since the Lord had prevented nonconforming ministers from guiding their flocks in England, He wanted them to serve elsewhere, and since they would have gone three hundred miles to obey the will of God, the three thousand miles across the Atlantic could not be allowed to impede the divine command. He then gave what was probably the most compelling motive for emigration. He stated that by migrating to New England, he gained the opportunity to practice all of Christ's ordinances, not just those permitted by the authorities of the Church of England.[17]

Like the other clerics who made the decision to leave their homeland for the wilderness of the New World, Mather's motives were not restricted to theological considerations. The possibility of incarceration, concern over actions that might be taken by the king, and the possibility of God's wrath descending on England were vital to all nonconforming clerics who made the decision to migrate. Yet to men like Cotton, Hooker, and other ministers, no one of these fears seemed to overshadow all others in their process of decision. However, in Mather's manuscript discussion, with its list of reasons for leaving England, he revealed that while preservation of the true religion and the desire to submit to the commands of God were a part of his thoughts, they were only a small part. Dominating his reasoning at every step was an all-pervasive fear for his own physical safety. At each point in his examination, worry over a revival of persecution in the manner practiced in Queen Mary's reign seemed to haunt him.

Mather's abiding concern over renewed persecution is easy enough to understand. Like most of his countrymen, he was educated on the tales of horror and agonizing death contained in John Foxe's *Acts and Monuments of the Christian Religion,* a sixteenth-century narrative of faith and martyrdom, and the accounts of those who suffered under

Queen Mary from 1553 to 1558 seem to have affected him more deeply than other nonconformists. Perhaps part of the cause for Foxe's ghastly immediacy was Mather's familiarity with many of the executions that had taken place near Lowtown, Winwick, or Toxteth Park, and his knowledge of local nonconformists who had suffered elsewhere. In his youth the persecutions directed by Mary had been a part of the recollections of living men, and there were many in his village who could describe events that had taken place in those terrible times. The list of those in Lancashire who had died for their faith was long, and Mather knew it well. There was James Abbes of Bury, Jeffry Hunt of Legh, the Midgeleys, father and son, Gosnal and Marck of Boulton, and Bourne and Bradford of Manchester.[18]

The account of the execution of John Bradford was especially frightening to Mather as he wrote out his thoughts on migration. Bradford had been executed in London in 1555, but his letters from prison were contained in the *Acts and Monuments,* and eighty years later Mather trembled as he reread the detailed narration of how the heroic nonconformist first kissed the stake, then turned to the man about to die alongside him and said, "Be of good comfort, brother; for we shall have a merry supper with the Lord this night."[19] Although the deposed minister of Toxteth Park only anticipated the possibility of a similar end, he could never, even in his discussion of "Removing from Old England to New," muster a comparable amount of bravado. His reasons reveal that he was a frightened man who had no desire to prove his faith on the gibbet or at the stake. Neither did he feel compelled to suffer physically as an affirmation of his love of God. He saw clearly the possibility of the Divine Wrath being directed against an unrepentant England, and here, too, his concern over such an eventuality seemed more intense than the fears of his persecuted colleagues. His reasons for migration were filled with biblical examples of the suffering that had befallen God's servants. He wrote of Christ being stoned by the Jews, the Pharoah's attempts to destroy Moses, and the fate of Sodom and Gomorrah, and always, as he contemplated these and even greater horrors, the words of Proverbs 22:3 kept returning to him: "A prudent man forseeth the evil, and hideth himself: but the simple pass on, and are punished."

Richard Mather's *Journal*

On April 16, 1635, the day when he set out with his family for North America, Richard Mather began a journal.[20] His record was a detailed account of the tribulation, frustration, excitement, and enlightenment experienced by a seventeenth-century English rustic on his first lengthy journey away from the neighborhood where he was born and had spent most of his life. The Mathers left the village of Warrington and traveled to Bristol, arriving on the twenty-third of the month. Richard's son Increase later reported the family had to travel in disguise to avoid pursuers much in the manner that Cotton and Hooker adopted to avoid those sent to apprehend them two years earlier, but a clandestine trip from Lancashire does not seem to be borne out by the testimony of the minister.[21] He recorded in his *Journal* that traveling to Bristol was "a very healthfull, safe and prosperous journey all the way . . . taking but easy journeyes because of the children and footemen, dispatching 119 or 120 miles in seven dayes" (5).

Mather's later *Journal* entries reflected the amazement of a landsman on his first ocean voyage. He wrote of winds and tide and drunken sailors, and described the delight of the travelers at the antics of a school of porpoises that dove and frolicked about the ship. He was fascinated by the sea creatures he observed, and explained, after seeing a school of whales spewing vapor, that they had undoubtedly been sent by God to reaffirm his faith for it was only after observing one of the monsters that he realized how Jonah actually could have lived in the stomach of one of the gigantic creatures (20).

Although there were occasional moments of excitement, the weeks the Mathers spent at sea were largely uneventful, and the irregular entries in the *Journal* reflected the sameness of the days on the Atlantic. Mather noted that the ship left England with over one hundred passengers and crew members and, despite the long voyage, not one of them died. He wrote of a woman and her child who came down with scurvey and discussed an assortment of diseases contracted by fellow voyagers. As for the Mathers, Richard described their seasickness but he recorded that the family experienced no serious illness during the crossing. The only danger the travelers encountered came in the last days of the voyage when the ship was caught in a hurricane.[22] The storm caused the company some hours of terror, but when it abated, they sailed on to Boston. Their voyage ended on the night of August 16, 1635, when their ship "came . . . to ancre . . . and so rested that night with glad and thankefull hearts that God had put an end to [the] long journey, being 1000 leagues, that is 3000 miles English, over one of the greatest seas in the world."[23]

On the seventeenth of August the passengers disembarked, and although the trip across the ocean was over for the Mathers, their travels had not yet come to an end.

Chapter Two
The Massachusetts Bay Colony

If Mather had hoped to find peace and accord when he arrived in New England, he must have been sorely disappointed after landing at Boston, for instead of the anticipated harmony among God's people, he found serious disagreement over matters of church government and doctrine. The difficulties plaguing the colony were not new in 1635 when Mather disembarked in America. They had begun almost as soon as the first settlers arrived in Massachusetts Bay five years earlier. Basic to the unsettled state of the colony was the reversal of roles experienced by the nonconformists who had migrated from England. In the mother country they had functioned in opposition to the established order, and though the intensity of their opposition varied in response to religious and political conditions, over a span of seven decades they had evolved highly sophisticated techniques of dissent. To perpetuate their movement for reform, they constructed effective systems for communicating among themselves, criticizing the Church, evading the will of the hierarchy, and propagating their own particular version of Christ's word. Their defiance of archbishop and king had taken many forms ranging from the persuasion and conspiracy common under Elizabeth and James I to more open defiance during the reign of Charles I. By the time of Mather's problems with the authorities, nonconformists had gained influence on some levels of the English church far out of proportion to the positions they occupied as ordinary clerics. Their ability to gain Mather's reinstatement the first time he was suspended was only one example of their activities, and John Cotton's reliance on the influence of religious sympathizers to protect him while he preached was so well known that one of his fellow ministers, Samuel Ward of Ipswich, was moved to remark, "Of all men in the world I envy Mr. Cotton . . . most; for he doth nothing in way of conformity, and yet hath his liberty, and I do everything that way, and cannot enjoy mine."[1]

By the time Charles I ascended the throne, the ranks of nonconformists had grown, and the new king was forced to adopt a program of repression to insure the success of his increasingly rigid ecclesiastical policies. The wave of persecution that resulted from his directives was the immediate cause of many decisions to emigrate. One group, for whom the burden of zealous archbishops and their functionaries had become too great, left England in 1630 and established the Massachusetts Bay Colony in America. The colony prospered and the settlers rejoiced in their newly found liberty to worship God in the manner they thought consistent with His commands, but while English restrictions on their religious beliefs no longer had to be opposed, they were confronted with challenges of equal magnitude. On arriving in America, they found themselves no longer dissenters but forced to assume the same position in colonial society that was held by both church and state in England. In Massachusetts Bay the colonists were now responsible for developing and maintaining the civil and ecclesiastical order. They were automatically transformed to a defensive posture by virtue of migration, and from the moment of their landing they could no longer enjoy the luxury of engaging in constant criticism; the settlers were in a position where they were forced to find solutions to the complexities of human organization and defend them rather than object to the works of others.

Complicating matters further for those charged with the responsibility of building a viable society from a group of immigrants was the mission they chose for themselves, to build a community in accord with the will of God. Neither their civil government nor their churches could be mere imitations of those in England with their attendant corruptions; they had to reflect the ordinances of the Lord. Yet in creating the secular government of their Christian order, the new arrivals were not free to erect any system they desired. They were restricted not only by the limited measure of control that could be exercised from the homeland but by the requirements of the local situation and the fact that those they were to rule were men raised within the English pattern of government and law. This alone would have made the task difficult, but the realities of a new continent and a hostile environment would create complications the leaders of the Massachusetts Bay Colony could never have imagined.

The complexity of organizing their churches, building a state, and all the while obeying the commands of God was a difficult undertaking, but the settlers made rapid progress, and by the time Mather arrived, most of the problems of civil government had been effectively met even though several serious ecclesiastical questions remained to be resolved. The specific nature of the religious discord was due, in large measure, to a theoretical rather than a functional bent that years of opposition from within the established church had given to segments of English nonconformity. For decades, nonconformists had explored questions of doctrine and polity (the term they occasionally used for church government), but the discussions were carried on within the organizational framework of the Church of England. Supported by this sturdy edifice, dissenters were able to study all aspects of the relationship between crown and church, experiment informally, unofficially, and usually ineffectively with ecclesiastical organization, and discuss grace, faith, and salvation with the desire, but not the immediate need, to compromise their differences. By the closing years of the sixteenth century and later under the first Stuarts, nonconforming congregations almost everywhere in England functioned within the established church, although rejecting many of its tenets, but supervision from state and church officials, despite its ineffectiveness, meant that there was no possibility of reforming such congregations completely. With the migration to America, the restrictions were removed. The settlers found that the vastness of the Atlantic conferred upon them almost unlimited independence in ecclesiastical matters, and they were free at last to build churches exactly in the manner ordained by Christ.

While they had hoped for a situation where they could worship without interference from English officialdom, they were not entirely ready to deal with it. There were many points on which general agreement could be had among the settlers of the Bay. All subscribed to the basic outlines of the Reformation and to a Calvinist view of it in particular. There was considerable support for a congregational form of ecclesiastical government, with each village church entirely independent from control by either a hierarchy of ecclesiastical officials or a presbyterian system of clerical councils.[2] Numerous other points were widely approved by the colonists: the *Book of Common Prayer* would have no standing in Massachusetts Bay; vestments, kneeling for communion, and a host of ceremonial procedures were proscribed. Still, within this outline of agreement there were many matters to be resolved. It was in trying to discern the will of God on these disputed questions of organization and theology that disruption surfaced.

In the Massachusetts Bay Colony, failure to achieve accord on religious questions was not something that could be confined to the academic disputes of a handful of theologians. To most of the settlers, the omniscience of God was not a glib assertion to be mouthed as the occasion demanded. His knowledge was complete, His power unlimited, and while certain aspects of God were admittedly incomprehensible, other facets of His character were impressed indelibly on their minds. Most clearly inscribed of all the features of His personality was an unequivocal nature. He was a God who wreaked swift and devastating punishment on those who deviated from His command, and He was mollified only when men lived according to His word. To ignore, reject, or disobey Him was to invite retribution more terrible than any could imagine. It would be visited not only on the man who defied Him, but on his family, his village, and perhaps his nation. Neither was this God a patient deity. Now that they had departed England and there were no ecclesiastical or civil impediments in their path, He demanded immediate compliance with His decrees. This was the only way disaster could be avoided. Unfortunately for the colonists, they soon discovered what generations of Christians and Jews discovered before them, that those decrees were sometimes not entirely clear and honest men of good intent often differed on their meaning. The lack of agreement was not the fault of God, it was the result of human failing. If men could not immediately discern what the Scriptures said, they must labor more diligently to understand them. Their lack of immediate comprehension could not be an excuse to permit disagreement or error to stand indefinitely while the search continued. God had prescribed only one way; that way had to be found before His limited patience was exhausted.

When Mather arrived in Massachusetts Bay, he soon found, to his discomfort, that the answers New Englanders discovered to ecclesiastical problems were often not the same as the solutions accepted by nonconformists in the mother country. He observed that this was especially true on questions of eligibility for church membership. In his native Lancashire where a presbyterial style of church government was accepted among nonconformists, membership was open to all who resided in the parish except for the openly scandalous or reprobate. This was not the case in Boston. The divergent practices in the colony were the result of differing nonconformist interpretations of predestination and the relationship of these interpretations to the church. Both English and Bay Colony Puritans held that all men were either saved or damned not as a result of any actions on their own part, but because God had chosen only some to be saved and had thereby condemned the remainder to eternal damnation. In the homeland the distinction between the elect and the reprobate was clearly understood, but since there was little possibility of distinguishing accurately between saved and damned, all who were not of scandalous demeanor were admitted to Church of England congregations, even those that were made up of dissenters from established practice. Among nonconformists, with the exception of those few who had separated from the established church, this system presented no serious problem. Saved and damned regularly shared fellowship and communion, and if this made some men uncomfortable, there was no remedy for them. It seemed that little could be done toward excluding persons of doubtful election in a land where a degree of conformity and attendance at religious services was a statutory requirement.

When the migrants landed in New England, they brought with them the familiar practice of offering fellowship to all professing Christians who were of good behavior. It was not until several years after the first settlement that this practice was altered. There is only a limited amount of information on the change, but it appears to have been brought about largely through the efforts of New England's leading theologian, John Cotton. Even before he was driven from his pulpit at St. Botolph's Church in Boston, Lincolnshire, Cotton decided that God commanded the elect to be separated from the reprobate by some ecclesiastical distinction, and while still in England he devised such a system, a formula whereby those who had received grace were distinguished from those who had not. His plan allowed members of his congregation who demonstrated certainty of their election to be set apart by subscribing to a special confession of faith. The other parishioners, although they remained members of the parish church, were excluded from the elite fraternity.[3] The plan was put into effect and remained a feature of religious life at St. Botolph's until Cotton was forced to flee England. Shortly after arriving in Massachusetts Bay, he became a minister to the church in colonial Boston, and with the force of his considerable persuasive ability and his reputation as a leading nonconformist preacher and scholar, he was able to induce local churches to accept doctrines similar to those he had advocated and utilized in England. The colony's churches differed from St. Botolph's only in that there was to be no elite group set apart from the congregation by a special confession of faith. The settlers went a step further and restricted church membership only to those who could present sufficient evidence to signify they were of the elect. All others were excluded from fellowship.[4] Later, a congregational system of church polity was also established in Massachusetts Bay at Cotton's urging.

It was this restriction of membership that became a vital concern to Mather, for shortly after arriving he asked to be admitted to the First Church in Boston, and to his surprise, the members indicated they were suspicious of at least one of his doctrines and the request was refused. The problem, they said, centered on the significance he accorded his ordination at the hands of the Bishop of Chester fifteen years before. The Lancashireman was not the only New England cleric who had been ordained by a member of the hierarchy. This was usual for most of the first generation of colonial ministers, and any objection on this ground would have been wholly fatuous. Mather's difficulty was that he assumed his ordination in England was sufficient to insure his clerical status for life, but he soon found that in Massachusetts Bay this was not the case. The logic of the colony's congregational polity, where there was no administrative body or hierarchical official to control individual churches or exert any supervision over the installation of ministers, meant that each village church ordained its own clergyman. When Mather refused to accept the necessity for reordaining English clerics at the hands of ordinary colonial townsmen, the elders of the Boston church took his heresy as a possible sign of damnation and he was excluded from membership.

Refusing Mather admission was something he could not permanently endure. He had been a cleric for nearly fifteen years, religion had formed an integral and essential portion of his life, he had fled England to seek a safe haven in America, and after his arrival it seemed inconceivable that he would be denied the right to participate fully in the colony's religious life. He examined the problem, prayed, discussed the matter with church elders, but soon realized there was little he could do to alleviate his difficulties. After three months he capitulated and accepted the New England view of ordination. Even then, it is possible some of the elders were not sure of the sincerity of his conversion or his complete understanding of doctrine. They asked him to write his opinions for further examination before they would vote to admit him.

"Some Objections Against Imposition in Ordination"

In his disagreement with the Boston church, Mather had maintained that in the Bible laying on of hands was not done by ordinary mortals, as was the practice in the colony, but by Apostles or by men endowed with special spiritual gifts such as members of the Church of England's hierarchy or the Bishop of Chester who had ordained him over a dozen years before. When this objection had failed to persuade the Bostonians, he changed tactics and argued that ordination by the laying on of hands was contrary to the will of God. It was, he then claimed, a dead custom rather than a living ordinance of the church. In the Bible, he insisted, it was a rite of the Levitical priesthood, an archaic practice, and all activities of this nature had been abolished by Christ. Even though the second argument did not correlate with his earlier statement on the laying on of hands, since it rejected ordination entirely, Mather was not to be deterred during these early weeks in America. He insisted, after the rejection of his first argument, that since the Son of God did not revive ordination in the New Testament, it remained proscribed.[5]

In the manuscript he wrote to satisfy the doubts of the Boston elders Mather began the recantation by attacking his own first premise that those who used imposition during biblical times were extraordinary individuals. He cited the example of the presbytery that ordained Timothy to refute this. Maintaining the group was composed of ordinary men, he insisted that the presence of Paul among them did not alter his interpretation of the group's character. He reasoned that while Paul was, by any definition, more than just an ordinary man, the imposition of hands on Timothy was not the act of Paul alone, it was a collective gesture of the presbytery, and as such, it was the deed of ordinary men. The apostolic character of Paul was not significant within the context of this particular event. He further supported his contention by insisting that through the imposition of hands was used for a variety of purposes in the Old Testament, particularly for healing and performing miracles, the inability of seventeenth-century Christians to duplicate biblical miracles by imposition in no way interfered with or prohibited the use of the practice in ordination. The purpose of the act, as it was used in Massachusetts Bay, was not to heal nor was it to perform miracles. It was a symbolic act, he said, employed only to set a man apart and dedicate him to God in a holy calling (3).

In the second of his objections to the colony's doctrine on ordination, Mather had stated that imposition was no longer usable because Christ eliminated all ceremonies of the Israelites and he did not reintroduce the laying on of hands in the New Testament. When it became necessary for him to demonstrate the error of his premise, Mather relied on typology, a manner of theological disputation employing Old Testament examples as symbols for New Testament practice. By the seventeenth century typology was a familiar technique to all Christian theologians, but to Mather and his fellow nonconformists it embodied particular advantages. Although originally employed to give authority to Christian teachings by establishing a firm connection with the Old Testament, it was especially useful to groups who objected to standard or accepted doctrine. By using Old Testament events in prophetical anticipation of the person of Christ for their own particular interpretations of New Testament events and practices they could establish not only the continuity of Christianity for their parishioners but also the continuity of their own particular doctrine and polity. The swallowing of Jonah by the whale and his subsequent release, for example, was commonly described in the language of typology as an intimation and a prophecy of Christ's later entombment and resurrection, and similar linkings of Old and New Testament events were induced from hundreds of biblical incidents. In his typological arguments Mather, like generations of religious scholars before him, also explained that while Old Testament practices did indeed presage New Testament events, Christians must understand that the practices of the Israelites were not designed by God to serve as archetypes or models for men in the seventeenth century. They were not to be copied in all their details but were to serve only for the guidance of Christ's churches. This meant that although the Hebrews' use of circumcision anticipated Christian baptism, there need be no similarity in the outward form of rites that were coupled typologically. Similarly, he explained, the use of the laying on of hands by the Levites or by any Israelites in the Old Testament provided a symbol rather than an example for the use of a similar practice in New England. The model for the employment of hands in ordination came from the New Testament use of imposition by the presbyteries of the early church and by the Apostles.

In the course of his discussion Mather not only defended laying on of hands, he also presented an excellent analysis of the purpose of the rite during the installation of Massachusetts Bay ministers. In contrast with the practices in England but in concert with Bay Colony determinations, he did not insist that the utilization of the gesture was an integral part of ordination. Nonconformist doctrine maintained that it was not one of the commands of Christ and since it was not commanded it was not essential to the ecclesiastical equipment of a minister. Still, Christ and the Apostles had used the gesture and so should all Christians, Mather insisted, but he explained that it was to be used only to convey the orderliness and solemnity of the occasion, not as a means of communicating spiritual essence. It was merely a visible sign of the divine inspiration inherent in ordination rather than the vehicle for conveying the transcendental gifts necessary for pastoral office. The purpose of the ceremony was "to set a man apart, and to dedicate him unto God in an holy calling. . . . to impose the burden and chardge of the people, upon the person ordeyned . . . to be as a seale to approve and confirme the ministeriall gifts of the persons ordeyned" (3).

The explanation in the tract was sufficient to allay the fears of a recurrence of Mather's earlier errors. In October, 1635, he was admitted to the church. Later that month he dated the manuscript, added a rubric and the initials R.M. in strokes much bolder than the text; then, its purpose accomplished, he set it aside never to bother with it again.

The resolution of his difficulties with the Boston church did not conclude Mather's differences with the Bay Colony authorities. His next encounter began shortly after his admission to membership when he received invitations to serve at churches in Plymouth, Dorchester, and Roxbury. Being unfamiliar with Massachusetts, the immigrant found it difficult to choose from among the three, and once more he sought the guidance of those whose advice he had followed in making his decision to migrate, John Cotton and Thomas Hooker. Both ministers suggested that he accept the offer made by Dorchester. Mather heeded their words for the second time, and he and his family made preparations to move.

When Mather was asked to take the pulpit in Dorchester, the village was without minister or church organization. John Warham, the town's first pastor, had migrated westward to the valley of the Connecticut River with many of the church members, and his clerical associate, who remained in the village after the exodus, died shortly thereafter. When Mather arrived in Dorchester, probably in March, 1636, he was not the candidate of the church members, most of whom were gone, but he came at the request of those who remained in the depopulated hamlet. No religious body had been formed since the mass departure, and Mather was forced to organize a new church. This could have been a difficult situation for the minister, but fortunately this was not the case. Many of those who stayed were members of the old religious body, and divine worship was not suspended in the town even though there was no gathered church. Religious services were held regularly, and the only difference may have been that the sacraments of baptism and the Lord's Supper were not administered.

Accepting the bid made by Dorchester was not as simple as receiving a congregation from the Church of England, however. Instead of being able to step into an established pulpit, he was compelled to organize his own church. Further complicating matters for Mather was a law passed by the Massachusetts Bay legislature restricting the founding of new churches. On March 3, 1636, the General Court had found it prudent to require all groups hoping to establish churches to obtain official permission before they could conduct religious services. Approval was to be given by a council composed of magistrates and clerics from towns within the colony. To emphasize that any ecclesiastical body organized without conforming to the new law would not be recognized, the Court proclaimed that no person who was a member of a church gathered without the permission of the government would be able to vote or hold office in Massachusetts Bay.[6]

For several weeks Mather held religious services with his future parishioners, and then, in the early spring, he and his followers sought to obey the statutory requirement calling for each newly gathered church to be approved. On April 1, 1636, they assembled before the magistrates and representatives of the neighboring churches. The examination followed a regular procedure, each of the prospective church members going before the examiners, making a personal profession of faith, and testifying how God's grace was manifest in him. If the officials had any questions about the doctrinal positions of these individuals, they were free to question them on any specific matter. Normally, when they were satisfied that all of those who were to belong to the church were reasonably sure of regeneration, the church was approved. The examiners would then congratulate the members and extend their right hands in Christian fellowship indicating they approved of the presence of another "candle" in their midst.[7]

This was not the sequence that was followed with Mather's group, and after extensive questioning, the Dorchestermen were denied permission to gather their church. The stated reasons for the denial were not concerned with small points at issue nor were the objections on the part of the examiners merely superficial complaints. The church was rejected because the questioners found that a number of Mather's company had derived their ideas of salvation from theologically unsound premises. The questioning revealed that almost all of the applicants had not experienced a genuine religious awakening, as Mather did in 1614. They had erroneously based their notions of personal salvation "upon dreams and ravishes of spirit by fits; others upon the reformation of their lives; others upon duties and performances, etc.; wherein they discovered three special errors: 1. That they had not come to hate sin, because it was filthy, but . . . because it was hurtful. 2. That, by reason of this, they had never truly closed with Christ. . . . 3. They expected to believe by some power of their own, and not only and wholly from Christ,"[8] and some of the applicants confused the manner in which Christ saved the souls of men. With doctrinal errors of this magnitude circulating among them, the magistrates and the representatives of the churches who were assembled decided that though several of those who hoped to form the church had received God's grace, the greater number of the applicants had not, and they had no choice but to refuse the application. The board suggested that they defer their attempt to gather a church until some future date.[9]

The deep humiliation felt by Mather as a result of his ecclesiastical caning can only be imagined. These times of dislocation, journeying, and resettlement were difficult enough for him without added complications, but to venture a third of the way around the world only to find his cherished concepts of traditional presbyterial nonconformity were insufficient to reserve for him the respected position in colonial Massachusetts Bay that they had guaranteed in Lancashire was a trying experience. Still, the rebuffs he received were not entirely out of continuity with his recent experience. He might have explained to himself that these were incongruous times. Everywhere the traditional concepts of decency seemed to be giving way before an onslaught of grasping and covetous men who refused to recognize their stations and remain satisfied with them. The tendency could be observed on all levels of society. England was ruled by a king who dismissed his Parliament, harbored sympathy for the Roman Church, collected illegal revenues, and watched idly as control of the nation's religion was usurped by a band of benefice-seekers who courted the Antichrist, reveled in corruption, and harried godly ministers from their pulpits. It was an age when piety was persecuted and reformed religion was denounced.

Everywhere the ordered nature of society seemed to be crumbling as traditional concepts of reality were measured against the present. This was particularly evident to Mather after his initial experience with the Boston church, for, following his rejection, he began to see degeneration in New England, both in the abandonment of what were to him traditionally hallowed patterns and in the substitution of an altered ecclesiastical system at the behest of John Cotton, a would-be Calvin from Lincolnshire. The doctrine and polity of Boston and its environs in 1635 and early 1636 represented a substantial departure from familiar Lancashire patterns, and as the bearer of these patterns, Mather found himself conspicuously out of joint with the times. When he landed in the New World, he was a man of the past—at least the past of three years before—standing in the American present, a carrier of what had become almost over night a set of traditional values in a society consciously striving to abandon a corrupt tradition and build a community according to the will of God. His first impulse on encountering this situation was limited resistance and a petulant refusal to abandon previous tenets on ordination. After a short time he realized there was no viable alternative but submission. He bent to the anti-traditional pressures and accepted the Bostonian pattern, but it was only a matter of months before he was again a victim of the countervailing tendencies of traditional English nonconformity and Massachusetts Bay's particular type of divergence. He had organized his church hastily, without due regard for official insistence that it be rightly constituted, and when he presented his group of brethren in March of 1636, they were rejected.

Letters on Gathering a Church

In trying to discern the reasons for failure, Mather realized he was caught between the desire of the General Court to prohibit the gathering of deviant churches and his villagers who were anxious to have their church operative before any additional legal impediments restricted its gathering. Mather was also willing to accept at least a portion of responsibility, admitting in a note to Thomas Shepard, the presiding cleric of the nearby Cambridge church, that he was proud, vainglorious, and lacked sufficient humility to be a minister. But this was hardly convincing. While Mather may have been learning the uses of humility, he was not a humble man, and when the ritual self-deprecations were complete, he placed the blame where he thought it should lie, one portion on the government and clerical leadership of Massachusetts Bay and the other on his parishioners. Though he did not accuse the General Court of harboring nontheological motives in passing the law requiring official approval for the newly gathered churches, he did charge them with undue haste in approving the legislation, thereby denying him sufficient time between his move to Dorchester and the day he presented his villagers for interrogation. The other portion of opprobrium for the failure, he then noted, was with his flock, for it was their urgings that forced him to appear before the examining board prematurely. "They pressed mee into it," he explained, "with much importunity, and so did others also, till I was ashamed to deny any longer, and laid it on me as a thing to which I was bound in conscience to assent, because if I yielded not to joyne, there would be (said they) no church at all in this place, and so a tribe as it were should perish out of Israel, and all through my default."[10]

Despite his frustration at this second rebuff since his arrival in the Bay Colony, Mather must have realized after his mental flagellations, that only one course was open to him. Returning to England with a wife and four sons was an impractical alternative, especially since he faced the possibility of incarceration, and having been a cleric for over a dozen years, he was unable to pursue any other trade or occupation in a fashion commensurate with his Oxford training and individual aspirations. He had no choice but to bury his outrage and try once more to gain approval for his church. The retreat was made easier by Thomas Shepard who offered words of encouragement and by the biblical examples of David and Ruth who sought success and found it only after repeated failures.[11]

During the months after the rejection, as Mather conducted religious exercises with his parishioners, he labored to correct the errors of belief they held at the time of the April questioning. Hours of patient explanation were expended setting them right on individual points of doctrine and trying to make them understand the nature of predetermined salvation and why it was unaffected by a life in harmony with biblical demands. He explained to them, as he later explained the basic tenets of reformed Christianity to a later generation,[12] that some were chosen by "the decree of God or his predestination whereby of his owne free love and good pleasure he hath from everlasting appointed and chosen some certaine men to the obtaining of grace, and Salvation by Christ for the praise of his glorious grace," while for others "the decree of God whereby of his meere will and good pleasure some certaine men are not elected and ordained to life, but on the contrary are appointed to destruction or damnation to be inflicted upon them for their sinne, to the praise of Gods glorious justice." [13]

Remembering how he had been rushed to gather the church in the spring, Mather took his time for the second attempt. Almost half a year passed before the late summer day when he sensed that the group was qualified to make another application for official sanction. This time the extra weeks and months spent in instructing his people in doctrine were rewarded. The second interrogation revealed that the prospective church members were well taught by their minister. Now their answers contained no doctrinal errors, heretical beliefs, or misconceptions. On August 23, 1636, the clerics and magistrates of the Massachusetts Bay Colony were at last satisfied that the applicants were spiritually fit and they were allowed to join together in covenant.[14] In accord with the custom in the colony, Mather and those who were admitted to the church then signed their names to a written statement of faith and purpose, promising to "further ... the best spirituall good of each other, and of all and every one that may become members ... by mutuall Instruction, reprehension, exhortation, consolation, and spirituall watchfulness over one another for good; and to bee subject in and for the Lord to all the Administrations and Censures of the Congregation, so farre as the same shall bee guided according to the rules of Gods most holy word." [15]

A Letter to a Cleric in Old England

Shortly after his church was given official approval, Mather received a letter from a former colleague in Lancashire, identified only with the initials E.B., posing a series of questions about church practices in the Bay Colony. The newly installed minister replied with a long letter, answering all but two of the thirty-six questions that E.B. had asked.[16] The questions and answers provide a comprehensive picture of religion in Massachusetts Bay in 1636, and the letter also indicates that, after his series of humiliations, Mather was willing to suppress the pain and outrage he had experienced at the hands of the local leadership and champion the American brand of nonconformity to his former associates in England. This was particularly apparent in the lengthy discussion he presented in answer to E.B.'s questions on the procedure for admission into Massachusetts Bay's churches. Evidently rumor of the American restrictions on admitting new members had been carried back across the Atlantic and the complex and exclusive ceremony alleged to the New Englanders disconcerted many nonconformists in the mother country. In the letter requesting information, four of the thirty-six questions dealt with admission practices, and in his answers Mather felt it necessary to provide some of the longest and most involved explanations and justifications in his letter. His answers indicated that after his experience with the Boston church and his difficulties with the General Court over the qualifications of the Dorchester brethren, he now understood or was willing to accept what was required in the colony. When E.B. asked "Whether all that do outwardly professe christ, bee to bee receyved as members of a church rightly constituted, unlesse they give strong testimonyes of unsoundnes?" (85), Mather answered in a manner indicating he had abandoned the English view that all professing Christians in a parish be admitted to the church. He had come to recognize the validity of Cotton's arguments that churches must be composed only of those who could prove with a reasonable degree of certainty that they were of the elect. "Visible Beleevers are to bee admitted into visible churches," he said, "But they that professe to beleeve in it and do it in [illeg.], and not truely, have no right to church communion . . . and therefore churches ought to be carefull in trying the spirits of them, that offer to joyne themselves unto the church" (91). Still, Mather was not willing to make the break complete between the Bay Colony churches and English nonconformists with their advocacy of parish-wide membership. When asked if differences of opinion on church government were sufficient to prevent any from being accepted as members of a colonial church (85), he answered in the negative, saying "The apostle requires to receyve those that are weake in faith, and differ from us in opinion . . . and therefore no difference in judgement ought to debarre men from becomming members if the partyes bee beleevers in christ, and not pertinacious nor scandalous (92)."

The letter to E.B. was long and discussed many facets of seventeenth-century theology. Several segments of it were occupied with questions settled years earlier, but the reexamination of subjects where general agreement was a fact does not detract from its importance.

Not only does the letter provide an excellent indication of Mather's state of mind in 1636, but since it was examined and approved by at least some of his colleagues before being sent, it surely indicated to the local ministers that he was willing to accept their opinions and work with them to build Christ's community in the New World. When Mather returned the answers to Lancashire, he must have been pleased with his piece of work. It was ably done and its positive tone served to justify the correctness of his own decision to migrate for the nonconforming clerics who remained in Lancashire. Yet it is certain that, no matter what Mather's feelings were when the letter was completed, he never anticipated the difficulty and embarrassment his answer to thirty-six questions would create for him in later years.

Chapter Three
Defense of New England Religion

In 1639, after Richard Mather was comfortably settled in Dorchester, the Governor of the colony, John Winthrop, noted in his *Journal*, "About two years since one Mr. Bernard, a minister at Batcomb in Somersetshire in England, sent over two books in writing, one to the magistrates, and the other to the elders, wherein he laid down arguments against the manner of our gathering our churches, etc."[1] At the same time that Bernard's objections arrived in Massachusetts Bay, another set of questions was also sent to the colony by a group of nonconforming Lancashire clerics who were disturbed about several practices they had been told were carried on in the Bay Colony's churches. The arrival of the two communications from England gave the colonists an excellent opportunity to explain to nonconformists who remained in the mother country how in America they organized and operated their reformed churches in the manner prescribed by Christ. The desire to provide information about religion in the colony and to respond to the queries from the homeland were reasons enough to answer Bernard and the inquiring group of clerics, but by the time Richard Mather was asked by local ministers to provide the answers, other considerations were far more pressing than the desire to gratify or persuade British interrogators. In a decade of rapidly evolving ecclesiastical institutions, the need for a colonial statement of faith was immediate, not only to keep nonconformists in the mother country informed but also to provide a declaration of principle and practice sufficient to insure the degree of unity God demanded in a settlement dedicated to preserving true Christianity.

The production of a Bay Colony statement of faith was not an easy task for Mather. It was complicated by the substantial religious disagreements that had matured in the colony by 1639. One of the primary contributing factors in the failure to achieve union on matters of doctrine and polity was the congregational system of church government adopted in Massachusetts Bay. Although it was a system whereby each town or village church was an autonomous unit, answerable only to God for its practices and procedures and responsible to no king, bishop, or governing council, this did not mean that all in the colony were free to worship in any manner they might choose. The local clerics and most residents of the colony agreed that God prescribed only one way, and though deviation was permissible on minor matters, it could not be tolerated in more important aspects of religion. Heresy, deviation, and dissension were to be prohibited at all costs. The colony's clerics were not ignorant of the tendencies toward fragmentation inherent in their system of polity. They knew how men who went through the same experiences and training in England often harbored honest and irreconcilable differences even though great efforts were expended to reach agreement. In Massachusetts Bay the clergy moved in two directions to produce a system that would maintain ecclesiastical cohesion among the colony's churches. They first enlisted the civil government to aid in enforcing religious conformity and they supplemented the help given by the government with regular meetings where they discussed deviation and made efforts to compromise it to their general satisfaction.

An Apologie for Church Covenant

Unfortunately, neither the use of force by the magistrates nor the frequent discussions of ecclesiastical problems by the clergy were adequate to prevent disagreement, and so when Mather began to write, the works he produced were not merely answers to inquiries from across the sea. They were statements of faith designed to compromise severe local disagreements on matters of doctrine and church government. Nowhere was this more evident than in his answer to Richard Bernard, *An Apologie for Church Covenant*. Bernard was concerned about the Massachusetts practice of requiring all church members to subscribe formally to an agreement or statement of faith before they were admitted to fellowship in the Bay Colony's churches. The practice was not part of the ceremony of the Church of England, neither was it used by nonconforming groups remaining in England. Mather knew from his own experience that those unfamiliar with the covenant, as the agreement was called, would be suspicious of its divine authorization. He therefore opened *An Apologie* by carefully defining the covenant as

A solemne and publick promise before the Lord, whereby a company of Christians, called by the power and mercy of God to fellowship with Christ, and by his providence to live together, and by his grace to cleave together in the unitie of faith, and brotherly love, and . . . binde themselves to the Lord, and one to another. . . . as the Gospel of Christ requireth of every Christian Church, and the members thereof.[2]

After he had done this, he began to justify the employment of the covenant by using the Bible. The New Englander was aware that covenanting was an innovation peculiar to the colony, but he could hardly admit that this was the case. God did not innovate or restructure His churches, and the covenant could not be given validity as a recent revelation without creating insurmountable theological problems or denying much of what the Bay Colony ministers endorsed. Still, its presence spoke of novelty and had to be explained. Diffidently, Mather admitted that many changes had been made from the ceremonies followed by parish churches in England, but he justified them to his readers, and possibly to himself, by asserting that what seemed to be innovation was actually only the rediscovery of ancient and long-abandoned practices (32-33, 44-46). Referring to Cotton's use of a covenant for gathering his church years earlier in Lincolnshire and the failure of most New England ministers to employ a covenant while in the mother country, Mather said, "Some of us when we were in England, through the mercie of God, did see the necessitie of Church-Covenant; and did also preach it to the people amongst whom we ministered, though neither so soone nor so fully as were meete, for which we have cause to be humbled, and judge our selves before the Lord" (44). He then used scores of scriptural citations and Old Testament precedents to prove even to the most skeptical that the covenant had always been one of God's ordinances and that the colonists who rediscovered it should be praised for recognizing their earlier sins of omission rather than condemned for altering their practices to place them in harmony with a freshly discovered law of God.

Since hostility to various aspects of colonial religion was most pronounced among the thousands of immigrants who arrived in Massachusetts Bay over the preceding five years, one of Mather's most difficult tasks was to make them understand that churches in the Bay were still within the ambit of the Church of England, unseparated from the national religion in the manner of those nonconformists who had fled to the Low Countries or to nearby Plymouth. Restriction of membership, congregational polity, and the covenant all indicated the churches in the colony had abandoned the faith of the homeland, yet three thousand miles away with no bishop at hand to admonish him and no ecclesiastical court to remove him from a pulpit, Mather could not deny the validity of religion in England. Almost all who came to the colony in these years had not renounced or rejected Anglicanism or their English village churches. They had come only for the greater spiritual purity and temporal opportunities that Massachusetts Bay seemed to promise. Denying the validity of English religion was more reformation than they desired. It could only alienate them and endanger the colony by irritating an already hostile Charles I. If Mather's writings were to heal internal divisions without creating deep antagonism on the other side of the Atlantic, the only way to safeguard the settlement was to depict Bay Colony churches as vital parts of the Church of England, differing only in that they had instituted the reforms demanded by Christ.

Mather's attempt to please all and alienate none created logical difficulties for him since the refusal to deny categorically the correctness of the English church meant that within the homeland Christ's religion still lived. The Church of England did not utilize the covenant, hence if it was correctly observing divine command without it, there seemed little need for the covenant in New England. Mather could hardly admit this, and so after justifying the use of the covenant he was forced to demonstrate how churches in the mother country also used a covenant which, though not a part of their practices, was implicit in their ceremonies and as genuine as that used in the Bay. The reasoning to reach the needed conclusion was complicated and comprised the longest discussion of any single topic in *An Apologie*.

Despite its complexity, it was a necessary portion of the work. To
ignore the status of the churches in England was to give new arrivals
in the Bay Colony, as well as older residents who were excluded from
church membership, the opportunity to create disruption by leveling
charges of separation against the colony's churches. There was also the
concern felt by the colonists for the spiritual estate of those who
remained behind. Rejecting the validity of all churches in England
meant that Bay Colony religion was separate from English churches
and also implied that friends, kinsmen, and thousands of godly
nonconformists who had not migrated were placed among the mass of
men who did not live according to the word of God. Undoubtedly
some were of the elect, but if no churches were available to join with
in England, those chosen by God were being denied a portion of their
due and they lived in an external state scarcely improved from that of
the heathen. Abandonment of these people in such a manner was a
step further than Mather could safely go. Some means had to be
devised for assuring the colonists that their friends and relatives had
not been abandoned, and the implicit covenant, which Mather asserted
was present at least in some English parish churches, was designed to
placate this segment of potentially dissident colonial opinion. As was
the case with the whole of *An Apologie,* this reasoning was calculated
to serve a dual purpose—to provide a defense and justification of
Massachusetts Bay's religion for those in the homeland and to deal
with potential and present difficulties in the colony.

Throughout the discussion, while Mather labored at justification
and sought a viable compromise that would bring together divergent
views on ecclesiastical polity, he remained careful not to undermine the
value of the covenant either by softening its harsh exclusiveness or by
implying that somehow it could provide a way for those who were not
saved to become church members. He explained to those migrants
pouring into the colony who assumed that their English baptism might
entitle them to fellowship in New England that "Baptisme is a seale of
the Covenant between God and the Church, but neither makes . . .
members of the Church, nor alwayes so much as proves men to be
members" (32). New arrivals, used to the English church as it was
under Laud and Charles I, who might have supposed that they could
earn membership by careful observation of God's law were similarly

corrected. "If men in entering into this Covenant looke for acceptance, through any worth of their owne," he wrote, "or promise dutie in their own strength, they shew themselves like to the Pharisees . . . and turne the Church-Covenant into a Covenant of workes" (4-5). He informed those who remained in doubt about the right of some to enter into fellowship and the right of the churches to exclude others, "Those that . . . joyned were beleevers before they joyned. . . . for Gods converting grace depends not upon mans daring, or not daring to receive it" (19).

Since one main purpose of *An Apologie* was to heal internal divisions in the settlement, Mather did not indicate anywhere in his defense the depth of dissension the covenant and the Bay Colony's restrictive church membership aroused between one segment in the colony who accepted the practices as part of a divine order and another group that rejected them entirely. Instead, he wrote with enthusiasm about the practices and procedures that he had come to accept after his initial difficulties with the colonial churches. He also realized that the features of the covenant that made it effective in aiding some to assimilate—its exclusive character and the bond of solidarity it created among those who considered themselves reasonably certain of election—were the very things that made it the object of suspicion to migrants who were unable or unwilling to compromise or adjust their beliefs as Mather had done to gain membership. It was to these men who questioned the validity of the covenant that the main thrust of his arguments was directed. Cotton confirmed this when he explained to a minister who had just arrived in the colony from England that the scriptural justification for the covenant was proved by Mather's explanation sent to Mr. Bernard in 1639.[3]

Church Government . . . an Answer to Two and Thirty Questions

At the same time he wrote *An Apologie*, Mather labored on his answer to the series of questions sent to Massachusetts Bay by the group of English clerics. Since the reasons for the composition of both pieces were identical, it was only natural that there was little difference in substance between the two works. *Church Government . . . an Answer to Two and Thirty Questions*, was a bit more diverse in its subject matter and answered several questions that were untouched in the other effort, but like *An Apologie,* it was a discussion executed to insure stability in Massachusetts Bay. It presented an authoritative statement of the colony's procedures for admitting members to a church, the organization of congregations and their relationship to one another, the ceremonial and operational aspects of the ministry, and the colonial assessment of churches in England. The most noteworthy distinction between the works was the use of a question-and-answer format in one but not in the other.[4]

Although the essential purpose of Mather's two writings was to maintain cohesion within the colony by providing a model and a justification for church order, the stated purpose of the efforts, the need to explain the colony's religion to those in England, was not a reason employed only to obscure their real purpose. The necessity of delineating Bay Colony ecclesiastical practice for sympathizers in the homeland was an important feature of the works. The New England clerics were not foolish enough to assume that their observance of God's laws alone would be sufficient to bring England to the true religion. They knew they needed an active and devoted cadre in the homeland to continue the pressure for reform while they worked out God's plan in America, and so when Mather wrote, he attempted to explain how clerics in the mother country should organize and administer a reformed Church of England. It was not through intuition, he realized, that men would discover the composition and operation of true churches; it was by example, and Mather knew that the only nonconformists who had met the problems of organizing and operating their churches on a scale of any magnitude were the settlers of Massachusetts Bay. They had experimented, debated, struggled, and ultimately discerned the will of God. The next step was to communicate the results of their travail to sympathetic readers in England so that when the time came to reestablish true Christianity in the mother country, those to whom the task fell would not be wanting in the ecclesiastical technology even though they possesssed the necessary spiritual qualifications.

Mather was not foisting information on an unwilling group of recipients. Nonconformists who remained in England were vitally interested in all aspects of the Massachusetts Bay Colony, and they realized, as did the colonists, that effective coordination between England and America was essential for the aims of both groups. It was this interest in colonial affairs that was largely responsible for inducing nonconformists in the mother country to make inquiries about religious practices in New England. Those clerics who questioned the colonists were not men of eminence who, by virtue of their position, could demand a reply. Neither were they the officers of a hierarchy who had to be persuaded of the error of their way. They were, in 1639, ordinary nonconformists, village clerics like some of the colonists, whose interest and support were necessary if an alliance was to be successful. Mather knew the efforts he expended to answer letters and manuscripts from the mother country would reach more than one cleric or a single small contingent of ministers who posed the questions. Having come fresh from England, he was aware of the audience that would read his tracts. He knew that they would be copied and recopied by scores or even hundreds of hands just as he had copied Cotton's and Hooker's letters years before.

The questions and answers were part of a transatlantic attempt by dissenters to maintain unity within their movement and prevent dissipation of its strength by separation across a distance of three thousand miles. How successful this effort at cooperation might have been is impossible to ascertain. Had the situation in England remained static, perhaps colonial and English nonconformists could have achieved their reforms by working from within the established church, but this was not to be, for Charles I was not a monarch of limited ambitions. He was determined to overwhelm nonconformity, and he seemed to be making progress toward his goal in England, although this was not true in Scotland where reformed doctrine and presbyterial polity were well established. By 1639, it was clear to the king that if the English church was to be supreme in Britain, the Scots had to be forced to conform. This was not an easy undertaking. Unlike his father, whose years of experience had taught him much about the unbending northerners, Charles was more English in his outlook, and he reflected the traditional English view of Scotsmen, a curious mixture of distaste and contempt. Surely, he thought, a few swords north of the border would be enough to end the infatuation with John Knox and the Kirk. Events were to demonstrate that the Stuart king had underestimated the abilities of his adversaries, and after an unsuccessful campaign against the Scots, Charles found his army defeated and his treasury empty. The only recourse was to summon Parliament. In 1640, after an absence of eleven years, they were assembled, and the king found, much to his displeasure, that the funds required to continue the war would not be voted until concessions were made to the powerful nonconformist leadership of the body. Unwilling to bend to their demands for ecclesiastical reform, Charles dissolved Parliament, borrowed money from private sources, and in the summer set out once again to chastise the insolent northerners. The second attempt was less successful than the first, and as the summer came to a close, Scottish forces advanced southward into England. The victors were halted in their advance only when the king negotiated an agreement in which he made numerous concessions, including the promise to pay the Scots a large indemnity. With his army defeated, the royal coffers wanting, and with new and arduous financial obligations, Charles had no alternative. Parliament was again called into session.

The nonconformists now had the upper hand and reform of the church seemed imminent. The tide of optimism was immediately reflected by a drop in the number who migrated to Massachusetts Bay. Where over twenty thousand people had come to the colony by 1640, representing approximately three or four thousand families, the rate of immigration was reduced to a trickle the next year. Many residents of the colony, certain they were now safe to follow the commands of God in the homeland, returned to England knowing that once their country was purged of corruption, a new religious order could be built. After a decade of experience in the New World, the returned migrants were sure they had discerned the biblically ordained way, but it was far from certain that their New England practices would be accepted in the mother country.

It appeared from events in the homeland that the most popular style of nonconformity would not be that advocated by Massachusetts Bay or by the returned colonists, but instead the system adopted would be that used by the presbyterian Scots. Unlike the New England colonists, the proponents of the Scottish form of church organization hoped to establish a system of church government with a series of councils and governing bodies to superintend the operation of parish churches. It was necessary to reject the Bay Colony's congregational pattern of church government with no superintending authority if this were to be done. Neither could Massachusetts Bay's insistence on church purity or their required covenant be allowed in England. Large numbers could not be excluded from a comprehensive and nationally organized church, especially when many of those excluded had been members of the Church of England, either as conformists or nonconformists. The presbyterian sympathizers knew it would be politically disastrous, but more important, their interpretation of God's will prohibited it. By allowing all but those of openly scandalous behavior to become members of their churches, those favoring a presbyterian system were automatically placed at odds with the New Englanders in another area, that of intrachurch government. The colonists regularly allowed the brethren to participate with the elders in governing their own churches. With the Bay's restrictions on membership this was possible, but under the presbyterian system of open admission, control had to be lodged with the elders rather than risk decisions made with the participation of a relatively undifferentiated congregation. A further difficulty that set presbyterians against the New England way was their suspicion of congregational independence. Aware of the problems that were created by allowing each church to be an autonomous unit—and unaware of the ecclesiastical role played by the civil government in Massachusetts Bay—the supporters of the Scottish polity insisted on a hierarchy of synods and assemblies to adjudge religious disputes and make binding pronouncements on matters of doctrine and ecclesiastical government.

In 1641 and 1642 ministers in Massachusetts Bay became more uneasy as they watched the course taken by nonconformists in England. They carefully listened to accounts of the Root and Branch Bill in Parliament and heard reports of debates on episcopacy and ecclesiastical courts, and as they did, they became aware of the lack of influence exerted by the colony's example. The strength of the presbyterians in England did not presage automatic condemnation of the American experiment. There was a great curiosity about the forms, methods, procedures, doctrine, and polity used by the colonists. The English were aware of the colony's success with church and government, and while the debate over reconstitution of English religion was dominated by the advocates of the Scottish mode of church organization, when those who favored the New England system spoke, they were usually heard with interest and their ideas accorded respect. But advocates of colonial policies knew that they needed to persuade rather than simply to be heard, and it was at this juncture that Mather's writings on Massachusetts Bay's ecclesiastical settlement were pressed into service. The reason for their employment was the initial strength English interest in colonial practices had created for the supporters of the doctrine and polity favored by the Bay's clerical leadership. Hugh Peter, an influential nonconformist who had recently returned from America, was particularly conscious of both the need and the opportunity to popularize further Massachusetts Bay's congregational form of church government, and he obtained manuscripts of several New England works, added his own introduction, and, using two sets of typesetters to speed the task, assembled a curious tome. Printed to be placed on sale at Benjamin Allen's shop in Popeshead-Alley, it was not one book, but three consolidated into a single volume. The tracts were Mather's *An Apologie* and his *Church Government . . . an Answer to Two and Thirty Questions* along with New Haven cleric John Davenport's *Answer to 9 Positions*. Each of the pieces had been written four years earlier, and since the time of their composition they had circulated in manuscript among Americans and among nonconformists in England. Although the colony's domestic difficulties that Mather's two works were written to mitigate no longer plagued the settlement as severely as they had done in earlier years, his polemics were put to good use once more, this time to explain and justify the congregational system and demonstrate its superiority over the style of polity advocated by the presbyterians.

The effort by Hugh Peter to have the works of Mather and Davenport influence the English was not particularly effective. By 1643, those favoring congregational forms of church organization did not need a set of descriptions designed to effect uniformity among a group of squabbling colonial churches. They required an authoritative description of New England's predominant religious pattern.[5] This was a crucial consideration at this point because it was only through persuasion that the colonists could hope to determine the course of events in England. Mather's statements of religious doctrine and polity in the Bay Colony were written to still dissent on the local level and would hardly do for the present undertaking. The need was for a work by a cleric whose stature was widely recognized in England. The only colonial minister who fit this description was John Cotton, and he soon began to write a definitive treatise on colonial religion that would later be published as his *Keys to the Kingdom of Heaven.*[6]

A Modest and Brotherly Answer

Mather did not retire from religious disputation even though Cotton had been chosen to produce the book that would replace his works as the most widely available and generally definitive statement of Bay Colony practice. Although his limited reputation in England precluded his taking a substantial role in explaining Massachusetts Bay's religion in the mother country, Mather was determined to continue justifying colonial practices. It was only a short time after *Church Government . . . an Answer to Two and Thirty Questions* and and *An Apologie* were printed that he had his chance when a minor presbyterian polemic arrived in the colony. Awkwardly titled *The Independency on Scriptures of the Independency of Churches,* the slim volume was written by "Master Herle, a Lancashire Minister."[7] Charles Herle, the author, was an ardent champion of the Scottish form of church government and an active participant in the efforts to establish presbyterian forms of worship in England. His book was not a sweeping indictment of New England's congregational pattern but was limited to an attack on the doctrine of the independence of individual churches. He maintained that since all who wrote in defense of the congregational system said essentially the same thing, he did not need to direct his work to any specific colonial cleric or to any single New England treatise. Beginning with objections to the colonial assertion that there was no power in a council composed of ministers to command the obedience of individual churches to their pronouncements, he maintained that such church assemblies had God's authority to compel obedience, hear appeals, make decrees, ordain clerics, and excommunicate members.

Herle's work, coming as it did from the pen of an obscure cleric who possessed limited competence in theological disputation, was not a serious challenge to the New Englanders, not serious enough at any rate for the attention of a ministerial leader such as Cotton or Hooker. Quite possibly it could have been ignored by the colonists—and probably would have been—had not Richard Mather and William Tompson, the pastor at Braintree, both harbored a personal interest in answering Herle. Beyond Mather's determination to remain an active polemicist, the Bay Colony ministers had been acquainted with the English divine for many years before their migration. Herle and Mather attended Oxford at the same time, and their friendship grew either at the university or shortly thereafter when Herle became rector of Winwick, the village where Mather had attended grammar school. Mather's church at Toxteth Park was only a short distance away and the two men had many contacts during the early years of the reign of Charles I. William Tompson, Mather's collaborator, was Herle's predecessor as rector of Winwick.[8] With these close connections, the New Englanders took it upon themselves to correct the errors committed by their friend and fellow Lancashire resident though the weakness of the book made it no genuine threat to the colony.

In *A Modest and Brotherly Answer to Mr. Charles Herle* Mather and Tompson had little difficulty in replying to the presbyterian. The Englishman's effort was an unsophisticated endeavor and the colonists were able to reduce it to shreds not with complex argument or extensive scriptural refutation but simply by demonstrating its inconsistencies, contradictions, and poor structure. If Herle ever chanced to read a copy of the New England demolition of his work, he must have surely regretted his encounter with the two expatriate Englishmen.[9]

A Reply to Mr. Rutherford

After his rebuttal of Herle's *Independency on Scriptures*, Mather wrote another polemic against an advocate of the presbyterian method of church organization. His *Reply to Mr. Rutherford* was in response to Scottish divine Samuel Rutherford's monumental *Due Right of Presbyteries*. Unlike Herle, Samuel Rutherford was a major figure in the movement to establish Scottish polity in England and his stature meant that the work could not be ignored in the colony. He was a presbyterian of considerable reputation who had been educated at the University of Edinburgh, built a name as a theologian, and became a leading opponent of the degree of individual church independence practiced in New England. He had written extensively on church government, but differed from many participants in the debate over ecclesiastical order in that he sought to minimize the distinctions between the congregational and presbyterian systems. *Due Right of Presbyteries,* his major work, was important enough to be answered by a leading New England cleric, and Thomas Hooker was selected to write a reply. Mather's rebuttal to Rutherford was not a complete rejoinder; it only answered those portions of *Due Right of Presbyteries* that were critical of the answer he and Tompson had written to Herle. The complete colonial reply to the Scotsman's book was Hooker's *Survey of the Summe of Church Discipline.*[10]

"A Plea for the Churches of Christ in New England"

The responses to Herle and Rutherford were not Mather's most ambitious attempt to establish himself as a leading spokesman for the religious order in the Bay Colony. What he planned as his greatest contribution was a work written in reply to William Rathband, an English presbyterian cleric. The choice of Rathband's book, *A Brief Narration of Church Courses in New England,* as a spur to his major effort was unfortunate, for Rathband was an obscure figure, having little or no following on either side of the Atlantic.[11] His *Brief Narration* was another presbyterian polemic of insufficient quality to cause consternation among the Massachusetts Bay ministers. Nevertheless, it was a set of arguments that Mather was compelled to answer since Rathband, in building his case, had relied almost entirely on information garnered from Mather's *Church Government . . . an Answer to Two and Thirty Questions* and from the letter he wrote to his friend, E.B., in 1636 describing church practice in the colony shortly after he arrived. Though Rathband made a feeble attempt to keep the authorship of the letter anonymous, it was widely known in the colony that the initials R.M. used to hide the identity of the 1636 letter writer stood for none other than Richard Mather. To counter the embarrassing attack, the Massachusetts Bay cleric composed "A Plea for the Churches of Christ in New England." The scope of the work indicated that its author intended it to do more than repel a personal affront. The book was a lengthy tract that contained not only the rejoinder to William

Rathband but an expansive statement and justification of congregational doctrine and polity, sufficient in volume and detail, Mather hoped, to supersede John Cotton's labor in authoritativeness and persuasive power and to establish its Dorchester author as the foremost defender of colonial religious practices. Mather spent approximately two years writing and preparing the six-hundred-page manuscript for the press, but his careful efforts were to be wasted, for while he wrote in America, William Rathband died in England; Thomas Welde, another nonconforming cleric, published a shorter but fully adequate rebuttal of Rathband's *Brief Narration*; and the political situation in England changed sufficiently to make the expenditure required to publish the "Plea" hardly worth any result it might have achieved.[12]

An Heart-Melting Exhortation

In the same flurry of polemical activity that produced the replies to Herle and Rutherford, and probably consumed sufficient time to prevent him from making separate books out of the attack on Rathband and his extensive statement of faith, Mather also wrote *An Heart-Melting Exhortation,* another work designed to influence events in England. Written as an admonition to his fellow Lancashiremen, begging them to reform their ways or face terrible consequences, Mather clearly aimed the book at a wider audience, but again, as with the "Plea," this work brought disappointment rather than esteem to the author. By the time it was ready for publication, the opportunity to influence opinion in England had passed, and when the manuscript of *An Heart-Melting Exhortation* arrived in London, the city's printers, Mather lamented, were so occupied with other more important works that five years elapsed before it reached the press.[13]

Between the year 1639, when Mather composed his first important theological works and the completion of his answer to William Rathband in 1646, a radical change had taken place in the circumstances that motivated New England polemical writing. Although *An Apologie* and *Church Government . . . an Answer to Two and Thirty Questions* were addressed to inquiries and minor challenges from England, and ostensibly composed only to satisfy the queries and repel attacks from the mother country, almost every portion of them was a response to the internal requirements of the colony. Both of the works were part of an attempt to provide a doctrinal framework for a system of church polity that was a fertile breeding ground for disagreement, dissension, heresy, and ultimate dissolution. Even while the civil government provided the bonds that held the churches together, Mather, with the counsel, advice, and the occasional participation of members of the ministerial fraternity worked to fashion an outline of church practice that would explain, justify, and persuade all colonials, clergy as well as laymen, of the divine sanctions embodied in Massachusetts Bay's maturing religious practices. For the moment, perhaps, in 1640 or in early 1641, it may have seemed that Mather and the clerical brotherhood were nearing success. No difficulties had yet surfaced from Quakers or Baptists, dissent in several of the surrounding towns was not as severe as it would become, several minor disputes had been settled easily, and the agonizing problems surrounding baptism were in the future. There were some minor questions still unanswered among the clergy, but these were trivial compared to the disruptions just past.

Yet there remained England, and by 1643 it was evident that the only method for impressing a congregational pattern on the mother country was through effective argument. With this great task at hand, the techniques of persuasion had to be altered substantially. No longer could a locally respected but otherwise obscure cleric carry the burden of defending New England religious practices. His work could be used in an emergency, but the congregational clergy realized that to exert meaningful influence in England, the requirements were different than those needed to insure uniformity at home. The Bay Colony needed statements of faith produced not by an unknown minister but by men whose words would be heard and respected in London. The only way this could be done was to press John Cotton and Thomas Hooker into service to deal with the changed demands of 1643. They were both widely revered in the homeland, and the colonists knew the weight of their opinions counted for much among English nonconformists.

Mather never truly understood this. He assumed that when Hugh Peter selected his works in 1643, he had them set in type and printed because of their singular merit and irrefutable arguments—not simply because they were the only works available to fill an immediate need. When Cotton was chosen to compose the definitive work on Massachusetts Bay religion, Mather, rather than retire from disputation, sought out another adversary, and, with William Tompson, found a need to reply to Charles Herle. This was hardly sufficient to sustain him as a leading commentator on New England practices, for Herle's book was insignificant, poorly reasoned, ill-constructed, and the reply by Mather and Tompson was more in the nature of a denunciation than a rebuttal. Failing here to establish a reputation as a theologian, Mather again tried to refute one of the Bay Colony's detractors. This time he chose Samuel Rutherford whose *Due Right of Presbyteries* was already being answered by Thomas Hooker. Once again, the result was less than he desired. Mather's work was adequate to clear him from most of the personal attack to which Rutherford had subjected him, but even though he had designed the reply as a refutation in principle of Rutherford's book, it was not adequate for building or sustaining a reputation as a scholar of distinction. He needed a new and complete statement and defense of congregationalism written in the grand and expansive manner of Thomas Hooker or John Cotton. And though there was no need for another work of this nature, he set himself to the task. Unfortunately, circumstances forced him to combine his effort with the rejoinder to William Rathband's *Brief Narration,* but because of both the failure of the statement of faith to respond to any vital requirement in 1646 and the absence of any need for yet another rebuttal to the work of the deceased Rathband, the composite production found no audience, and perhaps it proved to be an even greater disappointment to Mather than his *Heart-Melting Exhortation.*

The failure of his polemical and didactic works did not dissuade Mather from further efforts. The political situation after the defeat of Charles I in the second English civil war and the actions later taken by Parliament to establish a presbyterian system of polity in England meant that there was little point in engaging in further transatlantic debate. Realizing this, Mather abandoned his efforts to produce the definitive statement of Massachusetts Bay church practice and set out to find a new cause to defend with his pen.

Chapter Four

The Dorchester Sermons

In the same years that he wrote in defense of colonial religion, Mather carefully attended the manifold tasks of a Massachusetts Bay cleric. Of those many duties, one which might have caused his thoughts to wander back to his student days at Oxford or even Winwick was the translation of several of the Psalms from their original Hebrew into metrical English. The occasion for the attempt at translation came in 1636 or 1637 when the settlers of the Bay Colony first realized the need for a Psalter that was uniquely their own. Until that time they had used the Psalm book composed by Thomas Sternhold and John Hopkins in the middle of the sixteenth century, but they had never been entirely comfortable with it. Like other nonconformists, they were exceedingly dissatisfied with the volume's many deviations from the original Hebrew text. A first attempt to remedy the lack of fidelity was made years before by Henry Ainsworth, the pastor of the English nonconformist congregation in Amsterdam. An accomplished Hebraist, he corrected most of the errors made by Sternhold and Hopkins, neither of whom were students of the ancient language. His new and annotated translation was adopted by his own congregation and by that of John Robinson in Leyden, and in 1620 the Ainsworth version was carried across the Atlantic to be used by the churches at Plymouth. The most convenient course for the settlers of Massachusetts Bay would have been to abandon the Sternhold and Hopkins version and adopt the 1612 Ainsworth psalms, but they were averse to using the same translation favored by the extreme nonconformists at Plymouth who had entirely abandoned any association with the Church of England. This alone was enough for rejecting Ainsworth, but in addition his metrical constructions were exceedingly difficult to sing.[1] The only solution was to prepare a new Psalter, and portions of the one hundred and fifty Psalms were assigned to select Bay colony ministers for translation.

When the work of setting the Psalms into English poetry was completed, it was printed at the new press in Cambridge and then distributed throughout the colony. It was adopted by almost every congregation. Almost immediately its defects were discovered. Not only was the book lacking in artistic merit, but many of the verses were hideously contorted to preserve the Hebrew meaning and yet jam the contents into an English metrical construction.[2] Although the numbers assigned to Mather are not known, those he prepared were done with observable lack of artistic skill. This much was indicated by Thomas Shepard, who could not resist the opportunity to poke a bit of fun at the lack of literary ability exhibited not only by Mather, but by his colleagues at Roxbury, Thomas Welde and John Eliot. In a short piece of doggerel he wrote:

> You Roxburough poets take this in Time
> See that you make very good Rythme
> And eeke of Dorchester when you the verses lengthen
> See that you them with the words of the text doe
>   strengthen.[3]

Preaching in Dorchester

The translation of the Psalms was an important project for the colony, but it was only one of Mather's activities during his first hectic years in New England. Although there were many such demands on his time, his most important task, as it had always been, was preaching the word of God. By 1643, his abilities in the pulpit were so widely known and admired that he was asked by the General Court to prepare and deliver the annual sermon at the election of the colony's officials the next spring. Mather did not disappoint those who had chosen him, and the Court was so well pleased with his oration that they ordered the printer "shall have leave to print the election sermon, with Mr. Mather's consent."[4] But the pleasure of the governing body was not without bounds. No provision was made to pay the charge out of the public treasury, and for that reason there is little likelihood the sermon was ever published.[5]

While his selection to deliver the election sermon was an honor of some magnitude for Mather, it represented only a tiny segment of his preaching burden. More than any other single activity, the preparation and delivery of sermons occupied the greatest portion of his life, and it was through the preached word that he had his greatest effect on those who heard him speak two and three times per week year after year. Since he was unassisted in the early portion of his American ministry, the authority of his words was undiluted by differing opinions, criticisms, or challenges from a well-educated and knowledgeable colleague. In the absence of any possible effective opposition from within his church, at least on the details of his theology, it was Mather's preaching alone, and not the writings or pulpit presentations of the Massachusetts Bay clergy as a whole, that became the vital element in the spiritual orientation of Dorchester and formed the conceptions of Christianity's workings shared by the villagers.

In preparing and delivering his sermons, Mather used William Perkins's *The Art of Prophecying,* the standard preachers' handbook for nonconforming clerics in England and in the colony. As Perkins instructed, exhortations in Dorchester were divided into four sections. Mather began with a biblical text, then "opened" the passage with several sentences of explanation, gave a statement of the doctrine contained in the passage, and then listed the numerous uses of the Scripture. After the roster of uses, he rhetorically added objections, answered them, and concluded with a repetition of his earlier statement of doctrine.[6]

Morning worship on the Lord's day began with a prayer and an exposition on a biblical passage. The congregation next sang psalms, then the cleric delivered a sermon lasting between three and four hours. This was followed by a concluding prayer and a blessing. After intermission for a noon meal, the afternoon service began. It differed little in format from that offered in the morning. In churches where there were both pastor and teacher, the duties in the morning and afternoon were usually alternated, meaning each man had to prepare a single long sermon, but since there was only one cleric in Dorchester, he was forced to compose and present two lengthy sermons for each Lord's day.

Preaching was not only a one-day-a-week activity in the Bay. It was the custom in Dorchester, as in many churches, to offer a weekly lecture for the parishioners in addition to the sermons. The lecture differed from the Lord's day exhortations only in that it was not accompanied by the full complement of prayers, psalms, and other activities. At his afternoon or evening lectures Mather preached the Gospel just as he did on the Lord's day, and the regular attendance of many of Dorchester's people not only at the lectures held in their own meetinghouse but at the mid-week orations held in neighboring villages emphasized their importance. Even Mather was not content only to deliver a weekly lecture to his own church. He often attended those of other clerics. A surviving portion of his notes for the year 1639 contains information on lectures by Hugh Peter, Thomas Welde, John Cotton, William Tompson, Jonathan Burr, and others. In all, the handwritten record includes information on sixty-two sermons preached within a period of only several months.[7]

It is often difficult to comprehend the intense devotion the colony's pulpit orators inspired in the heart of those who heard them preach, and although the imagery and direction in sermons of consummately able ministers like Shepard or Cotton still reveals sufficient passion to convey at least an intimation of what it must have meant to hear them from a meetinghouse pulpit, this is not true for the surviving sermons of most New England ministers. In the case of Richard Mather, especially, the attraction his exhortations had for the Dorchester folk who heard him preach again and again over a period of decades is not intuitively clear. But it is apparent from his surviving sermons, those that were printed as well as those that remained in manuscript, that the attachment was not the result of his literary virtuosity. Though a portion of the power normally accompanying a work designed for oral presentation is lost in a written text, any examination of Mather's sermons indicates they contained insufficient artistry to inspire or enchant no matter how forcefully delivered. In Dorchester the parishioners were not nursed on a diet of pulpit technique remotely resembling the ornate masterpieces by John Donne, Jeremy Taylor, Lancelot Andrewes, or any of the Anglican stylists of the century. Mather used little imagery or charm to hold his listeners, and on the few occasions when he attempted to add a touch of color or emphasize a point by using a keenly descriptive passage or one of the simple but powerful analogies for which nonconforming clerics were known, his efforts are wooden and unimaginative without exception. The best he could produce in years of oratory was a brief description of a monster birth in punishment for sexual misconduct and, somewhat later, he concocted the image of a riotous fellow condemned to the flames of Hell who suffered exceedingly because he "could not have so much as a drop of water to coole his tongue." Obviously neither these descriptions nor any of Mather's other artistic devices were of a quality that would place a congregation in his thrall. To be sure, there were legal requirements for attendance at religious exercises, and this accounted for the presence of some of the auditors, but neither compulsion or the traditional dependence of nonconformists on the spoken word explain the Dorchester villagers' devotion to pulpit oratory.

The dependence of Mather's congregants on the spoken word was in part the result of the functional position that preaching occupied in the village. During the preceding century sermons had become a driving force in English religious life largely because they reflected the interests, motives, and ambitions of the growing nonconformist element. In the homeland nonconformity drew a great proportion of its support from the new commercial and ecclesiastical classes who were yet unsure of their position in a rapidly changing society, for although members of these classes sought security and advancement within the established social structure, the church and the aristocracy were two areas where they experienced most difficulty in attempting to elevate their status. The traders and merchants were regarded with contempt by older established social groups, and the role of clerics drawn from the new classes was made more difficult when, as more and more of them came from the universities, the number of livings was not expanded to accommodate them. For nonconformists, or at least that status-conscious portion of them that came from the expanding and acquisitive class of sixteenth- and seventeenth-century merchants, tradesmen, and lower gentry, the sermon contained the necessary attributes to make it an ideal weapon for combating this exclusiveness. Unlike the Mass or the Anglican services conducted according to specifications from the *Book of Common Prayer,* the authority of the sermon was not couched in a specified sequence of mystical acts performed by members of a divinely designated elite. It was the word of God sent directly to man.

The agent of transmission, the preacher in the pulpit, was the possessor of no transcendent powers nor was he the appointee of a distant, aloof, and occasionally hostile hierarchy. He spoke not at the behest of king or bishop, but was the creature of his own church, often chosen by its members and serving at their pleasure. He stood apart from ordinary men not because he was a member of a priesthood and endowed with metaphysical powers but only because he had acquired considerable theological knowledge through the unmysterious process of years of study. The nonconforming minister was one of his own people, and unlike their establishment priest, he was not secured on a plane far above them. But more important than spiritual equality for the members of a nonconforming church was that they had not demoted the minister to their level; they had succeeded in raising themselves to the point where they stood firmly beside him, head to head and shoulder to shoulder. The effect of this, combined with the sermon that carried the implication that God spoke directly to man, was certain to offer an element of social security to classes singularly deficient in that quality. When Mather stepped into the pulpit on a Lord's day, he became more than a theological exegete intent on explaining God's will. He spoke the undisputed word of Christ. In his sermons there was no attempt to duplicate the precision of ecclesiastical debate. When he preached, he preached the commands of God, and like God himself, he spoke without equivocation. His oratory contained no hint of the theological disagreements that had almost created schism in the colony and had fueled civil war in England. It was direct, plain, and contained no latitude for doubt or disagreement. This was what his auditors hoped to hear: God's commands received directly, without the need to filter them through the representatives of those classes who labored assiduously to thwart their aspirations. This relationship was confirmed and strengthened by the nonconformist acceptance of predetermined salvation, for salvation through grace alone implied the devaluation of the procedures of Anglicanism with its sacramental, metaphysical, and institutional distribution of grace, and the corresponding elevation of the nonconformist preacher and of those upon whom he depended, his upwardly mobile, socially insecure parishioners.[8]

Beyond the usual quantity of doctrine and theology, exhortations to lead a Christian life, denunciations of Satan, assorted parables, and tales from the Bible, Mather's sermons contained an additional feature designed to build interest among the worshipers. He used his pulpit to expound on local issues. The intrachurch and intravillage squabbles that provided material for gossip and furnished the stuff that was of daily interest in the small, isolated community were included in his sermons. He regularly preached not only to chastise sinners and attack opponents on matters of doctrine, polity, and ministerial maintenance, but on one occasion he singled out a faction in the Dorchester church that was not sufficiently enthusiastic about paying him what was, by the standards of the colony, a generous salary. The town needed their minister, he explained, to bring them the teachings of God, the news of the birth of Christ, knowledge of His death for mankind, and assurance of the certainty of His return. He was needed to provide the necessary defense against Satan, his minions, and the misguided villagers who opposed the correct interpretation of Holy Writ. Another group who came under attack from the Dorchester pulpit were the Antinomians. Although the most direct assault from that quarter had been defeated with the fall of Mistress Anne Hutchinson and her departure from the colony, residues of her heresy evidently remained in Dorchester, as in other villages, and Mather was determined to extirpate them. It cannot now be ascertained who in his church harbored Antinomian ideas or how numerous they were, but the teacher denounced them roundly. This, in itself, may have made such sermons more appealing, but in small, closely knit populations like that of seventeenth-century Dorchester, the certainty that most, if not all, parishioners knew the names of those against whom Mather aimed his denunciations surely added interest to his words.

The aggregate force of such considerations goes far toward explaining the devotion to preaching found among Mather's flock. But in evaluating the total effect of these factors, it is equally apparent that there was more that brought his congregants to the meetinghouse for the regular Lord's day activities and the weekly lecture. The most essential single force in assuring a deep and abiding devotion to Mather's preaching, overriding in importance considerations of law and nonconformist social imperatives, was the doctrinal content of the minister's sermons. Mather left no explicit evidence indicating that he ever pondered the reasons for the fascination of his parishioners with

the preached word or that he ever wondered at the motives of those
who regularly filled the meetinghouse to hear him expound, but his
sermons indicated a careful concern for cultivating his audience. He
was vitally aware of the distinction nonconformists made between the
two parts of their congregations, the members of the church to whom
God had given grace and the remainder who, though excluded from
salvation, regularly filed into the wooden structure and took their
places year after year. Many of the Bay Colony ministers saw in the
two strata of worshipers the truth of the parable of the wheat and the
tares, and on at least one occasion Mather described the situation with
the analogy of the people at the Temple in Revelations 11: 1, 2 who
were welcomed into the inner court and the remainder who merely
observed divine commandments and could enter only the outer court.
This dichotomy explained to Mather the devotion of his church
members to the thousands of sermons they heard preached by God's
ministers. The grace within them kindled an irresistible desire to hear
God's word. The men and women could not suppress their divinely
inspired passion even if they so desired. As for those who had not been
admitted to membership, Mather's sermons reveal that he gave
considerable thought and effort to inducing their devotion to the
sermon, and the congregants listened to him year after year not out of
a devotion to tradition or a desire to gain status. They heard him
because he offered the most valuable commodity a seventeenth-century
New Englander could want: he told them of a way to gain salvation.

By preaching of a way to be saved, it would appear that Mather
gave support to the common assertion that most Massachusetts Bay
clerics were Calvinists in the closet and Arminians in the pulpit in that
among themselves they held that salvation came only through God's
gift of grace but when they preached they told of an Arminian type of
salvation through good works and a scrupulous observance of God's
commands. In the case of Dorchester's minister, this was not the truth.
In his sermons he gave the hope for salvation that is commonly
associated with the doctrines of Arminius, but at the same time he
built an elaborate casuistical pattern to imbue his hearers with a need
and a desire for justification by works that did not explicitly reject the
basic tenets of New England churches. For a man who counted himself
a believer in predetermined salvation, this was not an easy thing to do.

The suggestion of a way to be saved in a world where men were predestined was a difficult business, but it was a requirement of his Dorchester ministry. For Mather, like other nonconformist clerics, knew full well that there were few who could accept a clear and strict division between the saved and the damned, and that the human needs and desires of his congregants who were not recognized as within the visible church required more than mere acquiescence in a predetermination that would consign them to Satan for eternity.

"The Summe of Seventie Lectures on the First Chapter of the Second Epistle of Peter"

Mather's attempt to construct a foundation of teleological thought sufficient to provide acceptable psycho-spiritual support for ordinary men and women and at the same time not violate the doctrine of predestination was an involved task that could not be accomplished in a single or even a dozen sermons. It required years for Mather to unfold his carefully organized sequential plan of salvation. The pattern of development that stretched out over a long time frame was not a new form of preaching for seventeenth-century nonconforming clerics. Long before the first colonists arrived in New England, a plan, or morphology of conversion as one commentator called it, had become a part of English nonconforming pulpit oratory. The outline began with election or justification, the bestowal by God of His grace on those He would save. These individuals, through the manifestation of God's decision, were then aware of their impending salvation and knew their sins were remitted by Christ. The acquisition of purity through justification carried them to the next plateau of salvation, sanctification or the living of a life in accord with divinely prescribed teachings. This led to the final state, salvation by God. There were theological dangers created by reasoning from this morphology in certain directions, for if God chose some men for salvation and then ignored them, it could be inferred on one hand that there was nothing a man could do about his spiritual condition and thus he need do nothing about it. On the other hand, the assurance of election could erode all limits on personal patterns of behavior by creating a feeling of superiority to law and traditional conceptions of morality. Nonconformist preachers, in most cases, avoided these extremes by insisting that the elect must not only be prepared but they must continually seek assurance of salvation. They preached that avoiding the labors of preparation was a fair sign of reprobation while easy assurance of salvation was the mark of the hypocrite.[9]

In some respects Mather's morphology of conversion was similar to this widely used pattern, but it differed in that while the most commonly employed sequence was constructed in a direct and easily comprehensible fashion primarily to explain to the elect the mechanism for salvation and to guide them against heresies, the oratory in Dorchester was more complicated and circuitous, aimed at an audience whose needs were deeper but whose faith was not as securely fastened as the faith of those who had been accepted into the inner court. Mather's preaching made clear that for the elect there was the need only for preparation. Grace and election or justification were theirs, and this produced sanctification without the danger of Fatalism, Antinomianism, Socinianism, or any other heretical beliefs. The elect could gain great gifts from hearing sermons, but since their need to be guided by the preached word was not pressing, Mather was freed to direct the thrust of his sermons toward those who most needed the Word, the men and women who failed to offer sufficient evidence of regeneration to be admitted to the church. It was for them that his particular morphology was constructed. It was designed to explain how in a universe where salvation was predetermined and where some were already saved by receiving God's grace, those whom God had not saved might still gain salvation by living a life according to biblical prescription. As Mather knew, logic alone was not sufficient to resolve the conflict between salvation through grace and salvation by works, but this did not make his labors unnecessarily difficult, for in the end it was not by logic that he was able to convince those who were not church members that the gates of Heaven might well be open to them.

Mather was not the only New England cleric who walked a path between the grim finality of absolute belief in predestination and the Arminian heresy that by following a prescribed course of action each man could determine his fate. And like several of his colleagues, it was not merely the desire for congregational cohesion or a wish to spare parishioners a life of spiritual and psychological torment that drove Mather to find a solution to this set of logically irreconcilable premises.

Like other English nonconformists, he had a certain inherent revulsion for a doctrine that regarded the majority of men as condemned to Hell for eternity even though they attempted, to the limits of their capacities, a life in accord with that commanded by God. In an earlier day this unhappy doctrine had presented no difficulty for William Perkins who had provided the model on which nonconformists patterned their sermons. He admitted no vacillation on the question of election to intrude into his works. Perkins and most of his associates at Christ's College easily accepted the doctrine that all mankind had been damned as a result of Adam's fall. From that event forward, humanity was forever debased, and God could in no way be faulted if He had chosen to allow man to continue eternally in perdition. But though He might have chosen to do this, God was merciful to man. Some would be saved. He decreed, if only they would scrupulously observe the laws He had laid down for human conduct. Unfortunately, at least for those who had been unlucky enough to have lived between the time of the expulsion from the Garden of Eden and the coming of Christ, and who set out to try to obtain eternal life through this covenant of works, the restrictions imposed were so rigid that fallible man could not hope to observe them with requisite fidelity to insure salvation. God realized this and though mankind was hopelessly corrupt and demonstrably unable to purify itself, He relented and offered a new way to acquire eternal life. This was through a covenant of grace. Under this new program man was obliged to do nothing. Those who were selected for salvation were saved by God's gift of grace alone while the remainder of humanity was cast down to dwell with Satan. There was no way to alter what God decreed. Some had been elected, other had been damned, and nothing could affect the situation. This doctrine, adopted by Perkins from the writings of Calvin, admitted no qualification. Those who insisted the damned were condemned to Hell because God had foreseen they would be evil were denounced for trying to distort the divine will. God elected some, said Perkins, and rejected others for reasons that could never be known let alone understood by mortal man. Neither works, wickedness, love, devotion, or any other human act or emotion was a consideration. Some were saved and more were damned because God had willed it. Man was a token in the proceeding; it was God who decided. This doctrine was not a comforting one, especially to those who were unsure of their salvation. Most of the Bay Colony clerics had agonized over their own elections at one time or another, doubting and questioning whether they were chosen for salvation. Mather, too, had experienced doubts not only in his youth but on at least one occasion after his arrival in America. In his case, fears of damnation were later replaced by confidence in his own election, but for most who were unable to discern signs of their salvation in adequate number to keep them operating within the confines of their social group, something had to be done to mitigate the harshness of the doctrine of predetermined election without driving them into Fatalism or causing them to abandon Christianity.

Cotton, while still in England, had discovered a way out of the dilemma by giving his sermons a liberal infusion of the doctrines of Richard Sibbes, a fellow of St. John's College and a widely known nonconformist cleric. Sibbes was called a physician for the soul by his colleagues, and in the pulpit he strove to bring the saved a knowledge of their condition and to soften the aches of their periodic doubt. He devoted his preaching to bringing an awareness of their condition to his church members. His hope was to console weak Christians, and to do this he preached by implication what Perkins had condemned, a doctrine asserting that grace was widely distributed among mankind. Cotton, like Sibbes, was caught in the logical trap inherent in the acceptance of an omnipotent and omniscient god, but while influenced by Sibbes in trying to seek an escape, he ultimately arrived at a slightly different solution. Facing directly the issue of the damned, Cotton preached a more complete type of doctrine which included both segments of the Christian's dichotomy, salvation as well as reprobation. Though he was completely attuned to the concepts of free grace and predestination and avoided the slightest suggestion that faith and works could bring salvation, Cotton argued that grace was given absolutely to the elect, the result of neither faith nor works, while those who were damned were damned only conditionally upon the willful rejection of God's word either by refusing the means of grace or ignoring the knowledge of God. Men were condemned to perdition, Cotton taught, not by Adam's fall alone, but by their own sins, their abandonment of God, and their disobedience.[10]

Mather did not accept either Sibbes's doctrines nor did he move toward Cotton in his attempts to extend the compass of predestined salvation. Instead, he tried a different tactic. Unlike Sibbes who labored to plant assurance in the minds of the elect or Cotton who tried to inculcate the desire to strive for salvation among those who had not been elected by God's free grace, Mather based his appeal on the value of insecurity, the inability of anyone to discern with absolute certainty whether he was of the elect or the condemned. This was not an argument directed to those who were reasonably sure they were of the saints and had been joined to the Dorchester church. They had little need for such preaching. It was directed to those who were looking for assurance—the men and women who filled his meeting-house but were excluded from the Lord's table because they could not convince themselves, the church, or both that they were likely to be numbered among the elect. It was to these that Mather most often spoke from his pulpit.

Richard Mather's sermons held his congregation because they offered salvation, not through a denial of the doctrine of free grace and not because he adopted the techniques of Sibbes or Cotton, but because he was able to implant in the hearts of his flock the idea that every man among them might well be numbered with the elect. What had been rejected by Perkins, assumed by Sibbes, and avoided by Cotton was made by Mather to be the reasonable hope of almost every individual who heard his sermons. Some knew of their salvation, he said, but most could only wonder, and it was for those wonderers that he produced an elaborate casuistical web of circular reasoning, beginning with free grace and ending when those who had heard him preach stood and walked from the meetinghouse with the assurance that it was truly possible that they could be among those chosen to spend eternity at the side of God.

To work such rhetorical sleight of hand, Mather had to inaugurate his teleological sojourn at the center of the problem, the very nature of grace, but before he could prepare his congregation for edification on so weighty a matter, there was one necessary preliminary step. He had to persuade his hearers that there was the possibility of election for each of them. This was essential, for if the thrust of his preaching was to engender a feeling of possible salvation rather than to convince any man that he was among the justified, then none must hold that salvation was confined only to a conspicuous handful of saints. It would create only despair if salvation were restricted to the visibly holy, the likes of Winthrop, Cotton, or Mather. The Apostles provided the Dorchester cleric with a perfect example of the potential of every man for election and he explained over and over that among them were "men of no great eminency nor excellency in their beginnings [who were] fitted and called of god," and he supported his point often using the examples of Simon Peter, a poor fisherman; Matthew, a publican; and Paul, a tentmaker. The Old Testament provided even more material to illustrate the humbleness of those chosen by God, for here he could cite the example of the prophet Amos who was a herdsman of Tekoa, David who had been a mere shepherd, and several others whose origins were less than exalted.[11] This point was essential, for if Mather's auditors were in doubt about its substance, the remainder of what he had to say would be uttered with considerably diminished effectiveness. He drove it home again and again: neither poverty nor worldly condition were prohibitions against receiving grace; "there is none but god that knoweth who they are that are predestinated" (62).

After this had been established by regular example and repetition, Mather then moved on to his major line of argument, the exposition on the nature of grace or, more precisely, an exposition on the manner in which it came to man. He explained that grace was given by God without condition, as His free gift, the result of no action on the part of humanity either individually or as a whole. It was only after Mather had done this that his explanation was amplified, altered, and extended beyond the terminus established in Geneva for limits of divine grace. "The word of god," he added after delineating the immutable nature of grace, "is very plaine. . . . [God] will give grace to whosoever will receive it and come for it. . . . it is a great encouragement and comfort that the righteousnesse of our god will move him and prevaile with him to performe what he hath promised, and so to give unto his that grace of faith" (26).

This statement, and others similar to it, provided the breach that gave Mather his first opportunity to storm the citadel of inflexible and predetermined salvation. His seemingly heretical line stating God would "give grace to whosoever will receive it and come for it" might have made it appear that Mather was succumbing to the heresies of Arminius or Aquinas, but this was hardly the case. He knew that such a pronouncement could not be made categorically and then left to stand on its own merit in seventeenth-century Massachusetts Bay.

This was only a beginning, for the problem, as Mather explained to his congregants, was more complicated than simply appealing to God in prayer and requesting grace. Mere man could not approach God directly, but only through His son, and here again the matter was not as simple as at first it might appear, for though Christ was necessary to the salvation of man, the essential element in election, according to Mather's explanation, was faith in Christ. It was at this point that the needed qualifications appeared. In explaining the functioning of this relationship, he noted "The grace of faith as well as any other part or point of happinesse is the effect and fruit of Christ's passion; for he being lifted up (both upon the crosse in his suffering of death and in his ascension into heaven, and in the ministry of the gospell wherein these things are preached to all nations, being thus lifted up) he drawes all his elect to him . . . which is by this grace of faith there being no other way whereby we can come to Christ" (17). This, then, did not yet show the way to be saved. Mather had first assured his hearers that any of them might be worthy of grace, the essential element in salvation, but then, cleaving closer to the tenets of Calvin and Perkins, he backtracked and preached that while all might be saved, the only ones who were actually numbered among the elect were those who had been given God's grace.

Mather's problem, at this juncture, was the same that had been solved by Sibbes with his assumption of more broadly based salvation and by Cotton with his advocacy of conditional reprobation. Instead of following one or the other of these paths, Mather sought his own course and moved to attempt to instill spiritual uncertainty among his congregants. According to Mather, the link that followed grace in his chain of anticipation was faith. If the attribution of grace to some and not to others seemed arbitrary and capricious, then a rational God could be fathomed more easily if his listeners understood the integral part played by faith in the divine ordering of things. According to Mather's plan, faith was the ingredient that made predestination more comprehensible. "That none can be justified before they have faith or without faith is evident, because justification is after . . . calling . . . and consequently it is after faith, because faith is . . . in calling, as the answer of the soule to the calling of god calling to come to Christ and to god by him. The answer of the soule to this call is nothing else but faith. . . . so that justification beeing after calling, and faith comprehended [illeg.] in calling, it must needs bee that justification is not afore faith nor without it, but followeth afterward" (377). There remained, however, one condition and that, of course, was that faith, like grace, was not a quality inherent in man. If Mather were to concede that saving faith was innate even in some, he would be forced to deny the whole nonconformist position on salvation. Faith, then, like grace, came from God, but to let matters rest there meant that little progress had been made in communicating spiritual uncertainty and its complement, the hope for salvation, to the Dorchester congregation.

The next step was to add another quality and build once again, but to construct the next level out of a more comprehensible material than either grace, faith, or calling. These three quantities (or two if faith and calling were regarded as coincident) were, by Mather's own admission, impossible for man to understand. Grace was far beyond the comprehension of mortals; it was a divine extrusion without question. This seemed less true of faith, and perhaps some might even reason that faith existed more symbiotically with man than did grace. But when Mather equated faith and effectual calling to prevent his descent into Arminianism, the relation between grace and faith assumed a tautological character:

By calling is meant the first worke of God's saving grace, upon the elect in time afore justification, and Glorification . . . it is that worke of God wherein a lively and saveing faith is wrought and begotten in the soule. Election is that eternall purpose and decree of God concerning the salvation of some by Christ to the praise of his glorious grace. . . . The connection of these two, the one with the other is this that election is the cause of calling, and calling the effect or fruit of election. For whom God predestinated, them he also called. . . . and as many as were ordained to eternall life beleeveth. . . . and therefore faith is called the faith of God's elect. (254-55)

Mather then moved beyond this to explain how justification was indeed closer to man than God's whim. He added a new quantity, Christian knowledge, to his logical structure. Here he could illustrate for his parishioners using the Bible and pulpit to explain that Christian knowledge

Begetts holy longing desires after grace and the things of heaven. . . . As it was said of virtue that if it were seene it would stirre up wonderfull desire upon it self, so it may be truly sayd that the bewty, the fullnesse, the allsufficiency that is in God and Christ is such, that if it bee but knowne the heart must needs go out in longing desyres after the same. And if so, then that must needs follow abundance of grace, for when the heart is [illeg.] in grace desyres after these things, these desyres shall undoubtedly be satisfied; for so is the promise. (44-45)

. . . .

This holy knowledge is not without faith but is the begetter and bringer of it. . . . and if faith and humility, which are the means of all grace, if these be by means of this knowledge it may well be sayd that all things, pertaining to life and godliness are given by means of this holy knowledge. (58)

The implication of these passages was clear enough to Mather's hearers: knowledge preceded both grace and faith, and if some in his meetinghouse remained unsure of his meaning, he made the same point over and over again in sermon after sermon. Knowledge was the first thing given to the soul; it was the beginning of all other gifts. When knowledge was joined with faith, justification, and suitable actions, it brought salvation (42-43, 56-57).

Mather's manner of presenting holy knowledge to his auditors was similar, at least in several key aspects, to the pattern he had used to describe faith, but while he was forced to equate the origins of grace, faith, and calling as gifts of God, he failed to do this with holy knowledge. If he had done so, he would have been once again back at the point of departure. Holy knowledge was a breakthrough. This quality, unlike the others, was not an unfathomable commodity distributed in some mysterious and arbitrary way by God. The process of obtaining it could be apprehended by imperfect man. Thus, while Mather could have made it the gift of God, he did not. Instead, he conspicuously placed grace first in his morphology, then quietly preceded it with holy knowledge (available by man's own effort), then moved on past grace, adding faith, justification, and suitable actions to attain eternal life. Here again, the insertion of suitable actions provided a catch, but it was not as formidable as a God who dispensed salvation seemingly at random. It meant that after gaining holy knowledge, grace, faith or calling, and justification, only suitable actions (i.e., sanctification), were required. These, then, were the ends of Mather's string of logic, one end tied securely to holy knowledge and the other neatly wrapped and knotted around sanctification, two qualities that were at least partially obtainable by understandable human actions.

These two ends, holy knowledge and sanctification, were not only attainable qualities that contained the unachievable gifts between them, but, even more important, sanctification in a community accustomed to legalism and piety was a quantity or measure familiar enough to persuade almost all that they might be of the elect. In every resident there was surely some hint, some act, some dimly remembered Christian deed that might suggest, no matter how subtly, the presence of grace. The next step was to find enough sanctification to make it seem more likely, and here Mather provided a detailed set of guidelines. According to some of the acceptable signs he described, those who might assume themselves sanctified in some degree avoided conspicuous vices like "bravery in apparell above [their] estates" and instead were comely, frugal, and honest in adornment. They eschewed "excessive drinking, excessive taking of tobacco," gluttony, sexual excess in marriage, fornication, sodomy, and nonattendance at worship. Even too much relaxation indicated a lack of sanctification. This vice particularly disturbed Mather who noted that "The holy ghost speakes so much against excessive sleeping and lying in bed that wee may see here is also temperance to be used in Respect of sleepe," and he added, revealing the cause of his perturbation over immoderate snoozing, that "It is theretofore no small fault to sleepe unseasonably as in tyme of sermon and or prayer" (137-45, 146).

Such declamations against sin, usually lengthy and detailed, represented peripheral aspects of the logical continuum that comprised Mather's syncretization of Christian knowledge, grace, faith, justification, and sanctification, but they were used not only to illustrate certain points for his audience; they also provided a convenient opportunity for him to make lengthy and convoluted digressions, thereby disrupting the continuity of ideological flow and disjointing his presentation of the correct sequential relationship between the quantities in his morphology of conversion. With this technique, the preacher could reverse, reorder, confuse, and obscure the serried progression and logical connection of causal linkages (burying the alterations beneath a torrent of denunciation of impious conduct and injunctions to sanctification), and by doing this make it impossible for any listener to follow his logic. Once this was done, the sequence could easily be altered, and by rearranging relationships Mather was able to insinuate his message that man could be saved. He abandoned the morphological sequence that began with free grace and moved to faith or calling, then to justification and suitable actions, and instead explained, "Now sanctification is the means . . . of entering into the Kingdome of grace, and the kingdom of glory, and an abundant degree thereof, oh then let us strive after an abundant measure of all these graces of sanctification and holynesse, which wilbe followed with such an abundant measure, and degree of everlasting glory and happiness" (288).

The point of Mather's regular morphological reprogramming was to establish without explicit advocacy that grace could be obtained in a manner other than by the random action of God, a clear softening of rigid insistence on absolute predestined salvation. This was heresy if stated categorically, but lest he be challenged on this point by a visiting cleric or layman skilled in the intricacies of logic and theology, he was careful to cover his doctrinal flank by assuring the audience that "Perfection of grace and glory is through the knowledge of the son of god. . . . This knowledge is it selfe the gift of god" (56). The last statement represented a retreat from the ground Mather had been cultivating in preceding portions of his series of sermons. Still, to assume that this statement and other qualifying comments to the effect that sanctification could be had without justification or that "sanctification is the blessed will of God," reflected accurately his beliefs and that all of his previous reasoning was designed only for rhetorical effect or to complete a circle of logic is to misunderstand his purpose. In trying to discern what Mather's listeners understood when he preached this particular set of sermons between 1646 and 1650, the critical factors are repetition, elaboration, and emphasis, rather than a strict and careful examination of his sometimes confused and often misleading logic. The meaning of any of his sermons or lectures can be ascertained only by interpretation of the content within the form of presentation. This is not to imply that the correct approach is through interpretation not on the basis of what the sermons say but "by reading between and beyond the lines." It is instead to try and understand the effect of a large corpus of logically inconsistent material presented orally in small cohesive segments over an extended time period. In attempting to do this, it is essential to remember that the sermons Mather preached to his Dorchester congregation differed from his closely reasoned theological polemics. When he wrote to defend the New England way, he had time to revise, reconsider, rethink, and redraft countless times. His arguments were carefully constructed after lengthy deliberation, they were examined in their entirety, criticized by his colleagues, and the inconsistencies and incongruities of argument were removed or corrected. There could be no other way. When his works were read they would be examined for defects in reason or biblical interpretation that could be used to detract from God's churches in North America. This was not the case with his sermons. As he stood before his congregation none, not even the careful note takers, had time to weigh and evaluate accurately the significance of each sentence, analogy, or citation without missing his next words. There was no way for his audience to evaluate those points emphasized by oratorical technique against those pressed with minimal vigor by the pitch, intonation, and gestures of the man in the pulpit, and, most important, no man could follow his preaching over an extended period of time and examine and analyze the sermons as a unified and consistant body of thought or doctrine. But even if this could have been done, no examiner would fault Mather. If his sermons sometimes seemed to be leading toward heresy, he always retreated to safety, and if dubious points were made with great elaboration and meticulous attention to detail, he always clarified them or brought them in line with accepted ideology by a concluding sentence or phrase. Who, then, could know or prove that the understanding that remained with the hearers was not that produced from a single sentence buried amid a cataract of words but was instead the more extensive and elaborate depiction of the path to salvation and glory?

Unfortunately, in reading sermons originally composed for oral delivery it is impossible to discover the manner and method in which oratorical techniques were applied to arguments, doctrines, and ideas, but to assume, at least in the case of Mather, that because his voice has been stilled for some three centuries it is impossible to discern those ideas driven home by his unadorned preaching from those that were passed over lightly would also be an error. It is here that emphasis due to repetition becomes an important tool in evaluating meaning. By studying his repetitions Mather's pulpit techniques become understandable, and a reader of his sermons becomes aware not only of what he said but of the totality of meaning in his preaching and the effect of that meaning on his listeners. In this manner, Mather's deviation from the rigid stand on predestination becomes apparent, for while a simple examination of his words and his logical continuum reveals an insistence on the free bestowal of divine grace, the involved, convoluted, and contradictory nature of his logic, when compared to his carefully reasoned polemics, indicates that Mather's casuistry was designed to confuse rather than to explain. He was not attempting to clarify, he was trying to insert serious modifications in doctrine without appearing to do so. Thus he was forced into his elaborate casuistical pattern, for only in this way, through extensive and complicated elaboration and obfuscation, could oratorical emphasis convey knowledge of the individual's possible salvation, avoid an explicit and coherent statement of content, and at the same time affirm the widely accepted nonconformist principle of predetermined salvation.

In this manner he used the sequential morphology of nonconformity to convey a message entirely inconsistent with his words. Beginning with proof that earthly condition was no bar to election, he proceeded to the divine grace given by God, moved on to faith, and here, while nothing occasionally that faith, like grace, was of divine origin, he regularly portrayed faith as something that was, in some mysterious and unexplained way—at least by Mather—imbued with the breath of human origin. He then denied this was the case and moved on to the acquisition of holy knowledge, the initial or penultimate step in the progress toward salvation—depending on which sermon one reads. This was the first break with the Genevan tradition. Holy knowledge, according to the cleric, was derived in two ways: from the study of the Bible and by "attending upon the publicke ministry of them that are sent of God to enterprett and open the Scriptures, and the milk of God contayned therein" (135). Through these twin instrumentalities, man could obtain the quantities necessary for salvation. Knowledge, according to the Dorchester interpretation, begot faith, faith—Mather would never state this but the extension of his reasoning required it to be assumed—begot grace. The basic quality, holy knowledge, was acquired through sanctification, and thus, as man strove to increase his degree of sanctification, not only by reading and hearing the Word, but by cultivating all other aspects of piety, he was moving toward justification. The sequence and causal relationships of faith, grace, sanctification, and holy knowledge varied from sermon to sermon, but one factor remained constant and that was the implication of the possibility that any man could partake of the glory by acquiring first either holy knowledge or sanctification. With this revelation the wall surrounding predestination seemed to have been cracked. This, however, was not so. Mather was aware of the ramifications of his sequences and carefully inserted disclaimers such as "This knowledge is it selfe the gift of god," whenever he verged on abandoning predestination (56).

Again and again he repeated the process, bringing his congregants to the brink of Arminianism and then turning them aside with a quiet, inconspicuous, and low-keyed word of equivocation. Much as with the reading of parables in Dorchester, during the first experience members of his flock learned the outcome of the story, during the second reading it was the message contained in the story that became significant, and the significance of the story increased with the increased understanding gained after successive readings. So it was with Mather's sermons. The end product of his logic was always known, but with each retelling of the progress from holy knowledge to grace, to faith, to justification, to sanctification, to glory, the process grew in importance and the disclaimers, appended here and there, faded from the minds of the audience, remaining only to protect the minister from accusations of heresy. Repeatedly the Dorchester villagers heard at length and in detail how they could ultimately gain grace through Bible reading, hearing the Word, and the practice of holiness. This was what they hoped most devoutly to hear and Mather provided it for them. If his occasional equivocations disturbed some, this was minor. They were small, infrequent, widely spaced, and buried amid the mass of rhetoric. His hearers could not reread the Lord's day sermons preached over a period of years even if they had taken careful notes. Mather's implicit message overwhelmed its qualifications. When his congregation took their seats in the meeting-house, they came to be assured that there was a place for them in heaven and to hear again an answer to the question posed long ago to Paul and Silas by a trembling jailer who asked, "What must I do to be saved?"

Chapter Five
On Church and Civil Governments

In the same years that Richard Mather labored at writing in defense of Massachusetts Bay's religion, dissenters from colonial church practice were able to combine the force of their dissatisfaction on two seemingly unrelated issues and mount an ominous challenge to the colony's predominant congregational way. As he had done in previous years, Mather played a major role in defending local churches against the new threat, this time writing to define and delineate the scope and form of church government in the Bay Colony rather than answering questions posed by ministers from across the sea. The two aspects of doctrine and polity that agitated or antagonized enough settlers to create a veritable governmental crisis in Massachusetts were the local method of church government that had no means within itself to enforce doctrinal homogeneity and the restriction of church membership to those who could convince their village churches that they were saved by God.

The first of these difficulties, a congregational system of polity lacking superintendency by either king and bishop or council and synod, had proved entirely unworkable after a few years, and a pattern of civil domination of ecclesiastical affairs began to emerge in the colony. The process was well illustrated in the conflict with Roger Williams. After his arrival in the colony in 1631, Williams engaged in a series of confrontations with the colony's leaders. He quarreled with members of the ministry over the doctrines he preached at Boston and Plymouth and then with the magistrates over his appointment as minister to the church at Salem. Throughout the disagreements, the Bay Colony clerics attempted to persuade Williams of his errors, but true to their congregational system, they ignored the magistrates' request for a general conference to force the recalcitrant cleric into the locally prescribed pattern of conformity. It was not until after the matter had festered for three years that the civil government moved to find a solution on their own. The request by Salem for a grant of land on Marblehead Neck was denied because the town rejected the advice of the magistrates and chose Williams as their minister.[1] The General Court of September, 1635, then brought Williams to trial and convicted him of having "broached and dyvulged dyvers newe and dangerous opinions, against the authoritie of magistrates, as also writt letters of defamation, both of the magistrates and churches here."[2] He was then banished.

In trying to cope with Williams, the force of the Massachusetts Bay clergy, with all their arguments and admonitions, was insufficient, and the colony was obliged to cast about for an alternate method to restrict him. The pattern of church independence provided no ecclesiastical means to do this since the clergy lacked any degree of compulsive force. The General Court was the only source of sufficient power to solve the problem. The civil authorities stepped in to eradicate the difficulty and Williams was banished by secular authority. The expedient worked well, and the colony's leaders, having set a precedent, turned again to the civil government when difficulties with other churches made it prudent to restrict the formation of new churches. Meeting in March, the General Court decreed "it is therefore ordered that all persons are to take notice that this Court doeth not, nor will hereafter, approve of any such companyes of men as shall henceforthe joyne in any pretended way of church fellowshipp, without they shall first acquainte the magistrates, and the elders of the greater parte of the churches in this jurisdiction, with their intentions, and have their approbation herein."[3] It was this decree forbidding the formation of churches without official approval that brought Mather to grief when he first tried to gather a church at Dorchester, but more important than the problems the law created for him was the fact that its enactment was a giant step in the direction of extending secular domination over the colony's ecclesiastical affairs. Yet this instance was not the only example of the General Court's control of church matters that Mather observed in his first decade in North America. In the years immediately after his arrival he witnessed civil interference either directly or indirectly in church disputes at Salem, Piscataqua, Plymouth, New Taunton, Wenham, in his own church at Dorchester, and in other churches as well.[4]

Mather also noticed that the Court was particularly anxious to intervene in affairs involving questions of church government, especially after the successes in the English civil wars of those who favored a Scottish or presbyterian plan of church government. The growing popularity of the rigid and highly structured presbyterian polity, with its church synods, councils, and assemblies possessing power to make binding determinations in ecclesiastical matters, increased the possibility that those who favored a similar system in Massachusetts would gain support because the church government they favored was similar to that gaining acceptance in the homeland. The opposition to the congregational way, strengthened as it was by events in England, became even more dangerous when a group harboring presbyterian sympathies in the town of Hingham discovered a method that they thought would force the colony's leadership to grant their demands for a more tightly structured system of church government. They presented a petition to the General Court stating the case for presbyterian-style reform, and they added strength to their plea by including notice of their intention to appeal to England if the demands were not met. The Court realized the danger inherent in a petition to the homeland. If Parliament could be persuaded to take the side of the petitioners, the precedent would be set for continued English involvement in the civil and ecclesiastical affairs of the colony and the outcome of such intervention could not be predicted. The Court quickly crushed the threat with the levy of a £20 fine against the leader of the petitioners, but the victory was only temporary. A short time later another group of petitioners with both religious and political complaints sought to take their grievances against the colony's government across the Atlantic for resolution. This newest presbyterian threat from within posed the same twofold problem that the Hingham petitioners presented to the clergy and magistrates of the Bay. On one hand, the colony's leaders were determined to reject a Scottish type of polity and preserve their congregational organization, but they feared they would be unsuccessful in preserving their local independent church government if they antagonized a Parliament with strong presbyterian sympathies and thereby precipitated interference from London. Again, the General Court was forced to move, but by the time the second group of petitioners threatened to seek redress from England in 1646, the most effective course of action was not easily apparent.[5]

Part of the officials' confusion at this time was brought about by continuing resentment against the policy of restricted church membership. When Mather had written *An Apologie,* in 1639, he had tried to promote colonial unity by explaining the need for exclusive admission to fellowship, but he had not been successful in placating all segments of the community. The difficulty seven years later was not simply the persistence of the antagonism created by excluding professing but unproven Christians from the churches. The hostility of those excluded was heightened when they discovered that since they were not members, their children were denied the first sacrament. This meant that, as professed believers in Christ, they were raising unbaptized offspring who were spiritually no better than Indians or Turks who had never heard the word of God. The general hostility to the colony's government and clergy increased when those who had been baptized as infants on the basis of their parents' church membership grew to adulthood, married, sired children, but never were able to prove to their churches that they were saved and entitled to full membership. They, too, found baptism was denied to their children. The ranks of those who resented restrictive church membership and the denial of baptism to their families were joined in their dissatisfaction by new migrants from England who discovered on arriving in Massachusetts Bay that though they had once belonged to churches in England, in the colony they were denied membership and their children could not be baptized. The widespread dissatisfaction over membership and restrictions on baptism ultimately brought the dissidents into alliance with colonists who favored Scottish-style polity, for the presbyterians not only utilized councils with power to compel doctrinal obedience, but in their view each parish resident would automatically be a church member unless conspicuously scandalous and all members' children could be baptized.[6] If the two protesting groups combined forces and obtained support from England, it was conceivable that Massachusetts Bay might be forced to adopt a church polity similar in many respects to that in Scotland. If that happened, the dissidents' objections would be ended.

By the time the interrelated difficulties over church government, baptism, and restrictive church membership arose, the efforts to reach agreement were made more difficult by the growth of a feeling of uneasiness among the colonial clergy regarding expansion of civil authority. It was clear to them by 1646 that the churches were dominated by the General Court and that the clergy had never seriously resisted the expansion of secular power. The spectre of regulation of colonial religion by England was a frightening possibility to the ministers, but even more fearsome was the prospect of presbyterian petitioners receiving a successful hearing from local authorities. If those in the colony who objected to local church practices on polity, admission, and baptism were to persuade the General Court of the political wisdom and the divine sanction for presbyterian-style reforms, then much of Massachusetts congregationalism would be severely compromised. With the power the civil authorities held over the churches, this could occur if the steadfast support the General Court had given in the past did not continue, and with the growth of dissatisfaction over membership and baptism coupled with the increase in presbyterian sentiment this was eminently possible. By 1646, the fear engendered by the growth of secular authority in ecclesiastical affairs spread among ministerial leaders as they realized that the expansive powers of the General Court over the churches had to be restricted if the safety of God's religion in the Bay was to be assured.[7]

The Court and the Council

Like other members of the colony's ministry, Richard Mather had not always been suspicious of secular power guiding ecclesiastical affairs. Years before, in his *Church Government ... an Answer to Two and Thirty Questions,* he was willing to give magistrates unlimited control over doctrine, ceremony, and the establishment of churches in the colony. He had written, ''Who must have liberty to sit downe in this Common-wealth and enjoy the liberties thereof is not our place to determine, but the Magistrates who are the rulers and governours of the Common-wealth, and of all persons within the same. And as for acknowledging a company to be a sister Church, that shall set up, and practice another form of Church Discipline, being otherwise in some measure . . . approveable, we conceive the companie that shall so doe shall not be approveable therein."[8] There was no space for equivocation in this view, yet after the events of the early 1640s Mather was a changed man. His perceptions of church and state relations by the time of the synod of 1646 were substantially altered and he was moving in the direction of demanding strict limitations on magisterial authority in church matters.

The threats posed by disagreement over eligibility for membership and baptism, the worry over presbyterians, and the fear of English interference in colonial religious practice all contributed toward Mather's change of opinion, but perhaps the final incident that persuaded him that the authority of the General Court had to be restricted was the legislature's indecision when they attempted to summon a council or synod of religious and lay leaders to solve the colony's difficulties. It was a group of several clerics who requested the Court's summons. They perceived that the clergy alone would be unable to provide needed solutions, and they asked the legislature to call a council. The upper house of the General Court acceded to the clerics' request and passed the resolution, but the lower house, already deeply involved in a struggle for power with the upper house, refused to follow suit, and instead opposed the resolution. They denounced the action on the grounds that the civil government had no authority to call a synod or compel the churches to assemble. The legislative impasse created by the refusal was later bridged when the upper house consented to ask rather than order a synod to meet at Cambridge in 1646, but the damage was done. The bitterness that surfaced before the controversy was concluded made Mather and his ministerial associates realize that they were caught between contending forces and that no matter which of the two houses emerged dominant, the firm and united support the General Court had given the churches in the past would no longer be as certain in the future.

With the first winds of approaching autumn hinting at the lateness of the season, Richard Mather journeyed from Dorchester to Cambridge to join representatives from the other Bay Colony churches at the appointed work. The number present was small—perhaps indicating continued dissatisfaction—but the limited attendance did not prevent the September meeting from lasting two weeks. The participants discussed a wide variety of religious topics and agreed implicitly to preserve Mather's previously accepted 1639 statement of support for congregational polity where he said the colonists "dare not to far restraine the particular Churches as fearing this would be to give [councils] an undue power and more than belongs unto them by the Word; as being also an abridgment of that power which Christ hath given to every particular Church to transact their owne matters (whether more or lesse weighty) among themselves . . . . And for Synods, if they have such power that their determination shall binde the Churches to obedience . . . it is more than we yet understand."[9] The report issued by Mather and his colleagues indicated that, in addition to church polity, one of the foremost subjects of consideration at the council had been the relationship between the churches and the civil government.[10] The clerics, sensitive to the accusation that they were being dominated by the magistrates, strove to assert their independence. They carefully delineated the permissible circumstances surrounding the calling of a synod, and the magistrates and others who were concerned with the problem of the limits of civil power were informed that the General Court could call "an Assembly, and that for the same end that a Synod meetes for, namely, to consider of, and clear the truth from the Scriptures, in weighty matters of Religion: But such an Assembly called and gathered without the consent of the Churches, is not properly that which is usually understood by a Synod, for though it be in the power of the Magistrate to Call, yet it is not in his power to Constitute a Synod, without at least the implicite consent of the Churches."[11] If the meaning of this, with its inherent proscriptions, was not clear to some, the synod added, "Churches can Constitute a Synod without the consent of the Magistrate, although the Magistrate cannot constitute a Synod without the consent of the Churches."[12] Thus, despite the earlier assertions of a number of clerics that the General Court could summon a synod in 1646 as they had done earlier, the meeting rejected the action of those among them who had asked the General Court to call a synod and reserved that power for the churches. Before adjourning, the conclave instructed John Cotton, Richard Mather, and Ralph Partridge, a cleric from nearby Duxbury, to draw up models of church government to be presented at the next meeting scheduled for the following June.[13]

"Modell of Church Government"

Writing a decade earlier, in his answer to the series of questions on Massachusetts Bay religion posed by a group of nonconforming clerics in England, Richard Mather had spoken against the casting of written platforms of church discipline. Enumerating their defects, he said that, in addition to being unnecessary, they were likely to cause men to observe the external forms of religion while ignoring its spiritual and divine substance. Later, when he, Cotton, and Partridge were assigned to compose a form of church government he modified his position and labored unstintingly at his share of the appointed business.[14] In August, 1648, when the synod reconvened at Cambridge, they had two drafts of suggested church governments to consider. The first was written by Ralph Partridge who arrived at the synod with an abbreviated and meandering outline of church discipline. The other was Richard Mather's "Modell of Church-Government," a hundred-page manuscript statement of doctrine and polity that would later be adopted by the synod and published with their approval as the *Cambridge Platform*, the most influential of all seventeenth-century American ecclesiastical documents.[15]

The content of the drafts submitted by Partridge and Mather was generally similar, although Partridge's "On Church Government Written About the Time the Platform Was Under Consideration," was not detailed enough to serve as a model for the extensive statement of faith the synod hoped to produce. Partridge simply described in brief and elementary terms the type of doctrine already prevailing in the churches of the Bay, and he differed from accepted practice only in that he opposed the colony's congregational polity and suggested the adoption of a presbyterian style of church government. Those favoring the Scottish type of polity had already won some concessions in the preliminary report of 1646 where "Orthodox Presbyterians" were allowed to "stand together in peace and love" with New England's congregationalists if the "publick peace be not infringed,"[16] but the draft platform by Partridge indicated this was not enough. The Duxbury minister advocated a colony-wide presbytery which, unlike the powerful Scottish presbyteries, would be more in the nature of a synod with limited authority to compel obedience to its pronouncements.

Mather rejected the appeal for presbyterian church government in his own wide-ranging and full-bodied examination of almost every facet of the colony's religion. His "Modell" covered the whole of Bay Colony beliefs, administration, and ceremonial procedures, discussing at length subjects such as the general nature of the invisible and visible churches, the duties of pastors, teachers, ruling elders, and deacons, intrachurch administration, and excommunication. There was even a section on the item that occasioned Mather so much discomfort during his first months in the colony, the imposition of hands in ordination. This time he did not stumble on the issue as he had in 1635. Although the disagreements surrounding the laying on of hands had long been settled by the time of the synod, he felt obliged to devote two of his eighteen chapters to the topic and explain in detail not only for his colleagues but for himself the nature of the ceremony and its spiritual and logical justifications. The synod did not share Mather's need for so extensive an exposition on a subject well understood, but they accepted his description, reduced its length by half, and included it in the *Cambridge Platform*.

Mather's "Modell" was understandably influenced by the theology of John Cotton. The minister of the church in Boston had been the leading cleric in forming the Bay Colony's religion, and since most of the draft's content was a compendium of doctrine accepted after a decade and one half of settlement, Cotton's influence, sometimes in his own words, is to be found in most sections of the platform. Yet the "Modell" was not simply a restatement of what Cotton had said and written on previous occasions. Mather used the opportunity of composing a draft government to seize the initiative and move decisively to alleviate the colony's most serious ecclesiastical problem, the disagreement over baptism. In the two years since the summoning of the synod in 1646, he had been profoundly disturbed by the inability of the clergy and laity to reach an acceptable measure of agreement on the first sacrament, and much of his time had been spent in study and prayer for a solution. By the time he submitted his draft platform of church government in 1648, Mather thought he had found the answer. He now held that the Bay Colony's insistence on the purity of the church had been too restrictive and that there was ample scriptural warrant for broadening the number of those who were eligible for baptism. Still, Mather did not reject entirely all of the limitations placed on the number who could receive the first sacrament. He said only that there was divine sanction for baptizing the children of parents who had been baptized as infants but never admitted to complete church membership as adults. He wrote his newly acquired view into the "Modell of Church-Government," saying:

And further, such as are borne in the church as members, though yet they be not found fitt for the Lord's Supper, yet if they be not culpable of such scandalls in conversation as do justly deserve church censures, it seemeth to us, when they are marryed and have children, those their children may be received to Baptisme. . . . these their children are in the covenant, they may be received to the seale of the covenant, this being the mayne ground which other children are admitted thereto: and it is scarce reasonable and equall that these being partakers of the ground of Baptisme as well as others, that nevertheless others should be admitted and these be refused . . . reason requireth that these as well as others should share in the priviledges therein. (63)

Mather's proposed solution to part of the colony's problem over baptism received some support, but those who favored compromising church purity to alleviate disagreement over eligibility were not numerous or persuasive enough to carry the day. The synod rejected all attempts to expand the number who could be baptized and the completed *Cambridge Platform* contained no alteration of past practice. On this issue Mather had been defeated, but he knew, as did all of his clerical colleagues, that the difficulty remained and would have to be dealt with some time in the future.

Mather's humble and detailed treatment of ordination and his willingness to allow his solution to the problem of baptism to be expunged from the draft before it became accepted discipline might have indicated that he was a man at peace with his colleagues, the leadership of the colony, and himself. But the final chapter of his "Modell of Church Government" revealed a far different frame of mind. In the portion of his draft dealing with the relationship between civil and ecclesiastical authority in the colony, he abandoned any reliance on the work of John Cotton and struck out with the full force of his accumulated resentment, denouncing the subjugation of the churches by the General Court. When Cotton wrote his *Way of the Churches of Christ in New England,* probably in 1642 or early 1643, he placed great trust in the civil magistrates, even to the extent of involving them in the selection of ministers for individual churches. Describing the manner in which New Englanders chose their clerics, he explained that after a church had settled on a likely man, "They give notice also thereof unto the Governour, and such other of the Magistrates, as are near to them, that the person to be chosen meeting with no just exception from any, may finde the greater incouragement and acceptance from all."[17] He was almost willing to concede to the magistrates in congregational theory what they had already obtained in practice, the right to limit the gathering of churches. In fact, he probably would have given them this right without restriction had it not occurred to him that in both biblical times and later in situations where the magistrates were not Christians, there was no need for official approval to form a church.[18] Cotton was also willing to allow the state to correct erring churches, although he noted that when both church and state were "rightly ordered, and administered, one of them doth not intercept, but establish the execution of the other."[19] In his *Keys to the Kingdom of Heaven,* written only a short time after *The Way of the Churches of Christ in New England,* he continued to rely on the power of the civil government, but with less enthusiasm.[20]

Mather's 1646 statement of faith and practice rejected the dependence on the General Court espoused by Cotton, and there could be little doubt about the depth of his feeling as he wrote "it is not in the power of magistrates to hinder the saints of god under their government from entering into church estate, and therein observing the ordinances of Christ according to the rule of his word" (89). Surely when he demanded the exclusion of civil authority in so weighty a matter he thought back to that April day in 1636 when under a freshly passed ordinance he was humbled and humiliated by the magistrates who refused him permission to gather his Dorchestermen into a church. Now he had his opportunity to reply, and he used it to the fullest not only to deny the right of the secular powers to pass and enforce such an edict but to prevent them from acquiescing to local and English presbyterian demands and compromising colonial church purity by adopting the Scottish style of parish membership. He added to his prohibition against the restricting of new churches that it is neither "in their [the magistrates'] power to compell all their subjects to become church members, and to partake at the Lords Table. . . . We conceive it is easye to judge how unlikely a thing it is, that both these should be the will of god, both that the magistrates with the Civill Sword should compell men into the church and then the church and elders with the spiritt sword should keepe out, or cast out the same persons, whom the other one compelling or have compelled to come in" (89-90). Mather's opposition to the power of the civil authorities was not confined only to specific matters such as the organization of new churches; he also challenged their general superintendency of religion in the Bay, insisting:

It is not unlawfull for Christians to gather themselves into church estate, and therein to exercise all the ordinances of Christ according to the word, although the consent of Magistrates could not be had thereto; as is manifest from the example of the Apostles and Christians in their tymes, who did frequently thus practise, when the magistrates being all of them Jewish or Pagan, and mostly persecuting enemies, would give no countenance nor consent to such matters. And if it was then practised by them . . . in those dayes, and even under Christian magistrates, may [they] have the like liberty. For if these things were lawfull, needfull, and profitable when magistrates were enemies to the profession of the Gospell . . . the saints of God should bee loosers and in worse condition by having Christian magistrates, than if they had none but professed enemies, and so the arrest of christianity in the magistrate should make his power not cumulative, but privative to the church which may not be. (88)

To make sure there was no misunderstanding of his view on the role of secular authorities, he added that the magistrates had no lawful power to limit or restrict the churches and since their consent was not necesssary to make any practice lawful, there was no practice that could be unlawful through want of their consent (89).

Mather's reaction against the secular authorities was a full-scale denunciation filling a complete chapter in his draft platform, but the differences in the conception of his work held by his fellow ministers necessitated some modification before the "Modell of Church Government" could be approved by the synod. In writing his draft, Mather— always the defender of Massachusetts Bay's religion—was bent on producing an apologia for congregational practice, while the clergy and laymen in attendance wanted a more direct statement of doctrine and polity. To produce the latter, the assembly pared large sections of justification and argument and removed scores of the examples Mather employed to substantiate his every point. In the final section of his draft platform, the synod softened the tone of Mather's anti-secular polemic, giving moderate support to his attempt to restrict the power of the General Court, diluting his vitriolic sentiments but retaining his essential direction. The synod enthusiastically accepted his dictum that "It is lawfull, profitable, and necessary for christians to gather themselves into Church estate . . . although the consent of Magistrate could not be had therunto," eliminating only the gratuitous anti-magisterial sentence asserting that "the saints of God should bee loosers and in woorse condition by having Christian magistrates, than if they had none but professed enemies" if the General Court were to be allowed, as it was in the colony, to pass judgment on the qualifications of those who desired to gather a church.[21] At another point, when he spoke even more harshly and without a trace of equivocation, for the limiting of secular power in religious matters, they deleted the entire section, simply ignoring his pronouncement that "magistrates have no power from god to hinder [observance of God's ordinances] . . . And if they may not lawfully hinder therein, then their consent is not also likely necessary to make such practice lawfull before god. For how can any practise be unlawfull through want of their consent, who have no lawfull power by their dissent to hinder the same?" (89).

In another portion of his concluding chapter, when he spoke of the magistrates' power over church membership, the synod and the cleric were in accord in rejecting governmental authority in this essential area, but the synod was more subtle, saying only that it was not in the power of civil government to select church members, and they illustrated their point as gently as possible with the example of the

Levites who brought the uncircumcised into the sanctuary. Mather's blunt assertion that "it is easye to judge how unlikely a thing it is, that both these should be the will of god, both that magistrates with the Civill Sword should compell men into the church and then the church and elders with the spiritt sword should . . . cast out the same," was omitted entirely from the work accepted by the synod (90). This direct assertion was a bit too heady for men born and reared in a climate of secular domination of church affairs. Rather than accept Mather's unmitigated rejection of civil authority, they retreated to the safer ground of qualification and replaced his statement with a passage designed to soften the potentially abrasive attack on the magistrates. The passage, taken from Ralph Partridge's draft, retained Mather's substance but assured officials that "Church-government stands in no opposition to civil government of common-welths, nor intrencheth upon the authority of civil Magistrates in their jurisdictions; nor any whit weakneth their hands in governing; but rather strengthneth them, and furthereth the people in yielding more hearty and conscionable obedience unto them, whatsoever some ill affected persons to the wayes of Christ have suggested."[22]

Even in their rejection of civil authority, the synod of 1646-48 could not suppress their conditioned subjugation to the secular power as Mather tried to do. They refused to accept their own work as authoritative until it received the General Court's imprimatur. The document was presented to that body in October, 1649, but it was not immediately accepted. Instead the Court followed a more cautious path. After some debate, they elected to "commend it to the judicyous and pious consideration of the severall churches within this jurisdiction, desiring a retourne from them at the next Gennerall Courte how farr it is suitable to their judgments and approbation before the Courte procedes any farther therein."[23] When the objections to the completed platform were returned, the elders appointed Mather as head of a committee to compile a reply.[24]

"An Answere of the Elders"

Only a small number of churches and individuals took the proffered opportunity to object to the *Cambridge Platform*. Three churches, those of Malden, Salem, and Wenham, formally opposed some of the

Platform's features, and of the thousands of church members in the colony, only three raised specific complaints. Even though the number of objections was small, Mather could hardly have been cheered by their nature. While he was involved in trying to expand eligibility for baptism and had gained a victory in his attempt to restrict secular power, none of those churches or individuals who objected to the *Platform* seconded his call for expanding the number who could receive the first sacrament and neither did any demand further restrictions on the exercise of civil power in ecclesiastical matters.

Defending the Bay Colony's congregational pattern of church government was not a particularly difficult task for Mather. He had long familiarity with the arguments used by New England clerics over the past years in their disputes with ministers in Scotland and in England and he had used many of them himself in his exchanges with Thomas Herle, Samuel Rutherford, and William Rathband. When Edward Brecke, from his own village of Dorchester, insisted that "under the gospell not only congregationall churches, but also nationall and universall" churches existed, Mather offered a reply several pages in length.[25] He began by referring the questioner to the appropriate articles in the *Cambridge Platform* where it was explained that national churches existed before the coming of Christ but in the New Testament the earlier national church was replaced by individual congregations.[26] He then followed with analogies of "Civill corporations or many kingdomes . . . or many married couples, which have all like matter and forme," but remained individual entities.[27] Still, his most telling point was made by citing the existence of individual churches in the Bible. "The Argument [for congregational patterns of church government] is 'not taken meerely from the silence of scripture, but from the constant contrary language of scripture, which alwaies calls them churches in the plurall number, in one province though one of a narrow compasse. And some of our divines disputing this point against them of the Hierarchie demand a reason why the scripture should never speake in the singular number had those severall congregations in a Province ever bene a singular church" (6). He then followed with examples of the individual churches at Ephesus, Smyrna, Corinth, and elsewhere, none of which exercised superintendency over any of the others.

Many of the complaints about the provisions of the *Cambridge Platform* were minor, but in a statement of faith designed to express the accepted beliefs of as wide a segment of the colony's population as possible, all had to be answered. Mather was forced to explain in detail the tasks of the ruling elders in each church: again he justified the manner of ordination used in the Bay Colony, expounded on the relationship of the Church of England to the visible church, explained the procedure for moving from one church to another, and discussed the relationship between civil and ecclesiastical authorities. One subject that seemed of particular interest to the questioners was the precise nature of the sharing of power between the elders and the members of each church. In the presbyterian type of nonconforming churches in England, the leaders of the congregations usually made all policy determinations, but in Massachusetts Bay, where church membership was restricted only to the saved, the reliability of most of those admitted meant that the powers of ecclesiastical government could be distributed widely among the members. Still, the diffusion of governmental authority to the brethren, while discussed frequently in several expositions on New England religion, was not completely understood and accepted among either the clergy or laity. Mather's response to questions on the subject was vague and equivocal, indicating that he, too, was in doubt on many of the details and justifications for the local method for intrachurch government, but when forced at one point to make a clear declaration of principle, he said, "Elders are expressly called Rulers, and Leaders in the name of Christ, and the people are enjoyned to obey them and submit themselves ... Now it is the power of all Leaders, as Captaynes etc. to set all in their order, to give the word and command silence" (19). Mather's affirmation of the power of the leadership over the brethren went further than many in the colony would have preferred, but at this point the dispute over intrachurch government was a minor matter, and it would not be until many years later that Dorchester's cleric would be faced by a revolt in his own church over the issue.

When the *Platform* and the answers to the objections were returned to the court, the upper house unanimously gave their approval to the work. The lower house was not of a single mind. Fourteen of them refused to vote ratification. Two of the recalcitrants were from Salem and another was from Wenham—the churches of both towns had presented objections to the *Platform*.[28] Despite the protests of a portion of the deputies, the General Court thanked the committee for their service and approved the *Cambridge Platform* in 1651, stating that its contents were what we "have practiced and doe beleeve."[29]

The *Cambridge Platform* was a major achievement for Richard Mather. Although his invective was edited out of the segment dealing with the division of power between church and state, he had managed to carry his point. The synod was compelled to explain in detail its view of how the civil and ecclesiastical governments should continue working together, and their explanation was hardly a reflection of the situation that had evolved in the colony after two decades of settlement. Instead of English-style secular dominance, it was the Court that became the servant of the church according to the *Cambridge Platform*. Following Mather's lead, the synod stated that "It is lawfull, profitable and necessary for christians to gather themselves into Church Estate . . . according unto the word" with or without the consent of the magistrate. Eight sections then followed demonstrating that the elders clearly saw the state as a servant of the churches and not the other way around. "The powr and authority of Magistrates is not for the restraining of churches, or any other good workes" and though the task of the magistrates was, among other things, to assure godliness of the subjects, they were given to understand that this did not imply authority over church affairs. In ecclesiastical matters such as gathering, excommunication, eligibility for the Lord's Supper, or failure of a congregation to pay its minister, the civil government had no authority. The synod also accepted Mather's view on the method of forming new churches. The course adopted by the synod represented a singular departure from the 1636 practice, when the General Court had caused Mather so much difficulty and humiliation by ordering all who hoped to gather a new church first to apply to the civil authorities for permission and then denying political rights to those who were not members of approved churches.[30] In 1648 the synod rejected supervision by the magistrates entirely. When new churches were gathered, the *Cambridge Platform* specified only that "it is requisite for their safer proceeding, and the maintaining of the communion of churches, that they signifie their intent unto the neighbour-churches, walking according unto the order of the Gospel, and desire their presence, and help, and right hand of fellowship which they ought readily to give unto them, when there is no just cause of excepting against their proceedings."[31] Similarly, the clergy were no longer willing to accept interference in the affairs of individual churches. When the General Court entered ecclesiastical disputes in the 1630s, they had been welcomed, but by the time of the synod's meeting in 1648, all of that was in the past. Both Mather's draft and the completed *Cambridge Platform* included a set of procedures to correct erring elders and members, but nowhere did either document mention a need for assistance from the civil magistrates. The only issue on which the representatives hesitated was on the question of the power of the General Court to call a synod. They retreated from the position taken in their preliminary report of 1646 and conceded that the magistrates might call a synod. But even here they refused to surrender. They qualified their concession by adding that the churches could call a synod with or without the consent of the magistrates and, if need be, against their will.[32]

Richard Mather's "Modell of Church-Government" was an undisguised attempt to secure clerical independence from secular domination, and the statement of faith that emerged from the synod contained the essence, although it lacked the power and intensity, of most of what he had proposed. As a result of his bidding, the *Cambridge Platform* represented a major shift in the direction of diminishing civil superintendency of church affairs. The *Platform* did not prohibit the General Court from interfering in the colony's religious activities. Although rejecting civil participation in many areas, Mather and his colleagues wanted and needed the compulsive force of the secular authorities to enforce behavioral norms requisite in a Christian colony, and to retain this aid they included a succinct and specific list of cases where the magistrates' assistance would be needed for punishing idolatry, blasphemy, and heresy, just as they had done in the past. In cases of schism, where the churches first determined the rectitude of the course to be followed, the Court would be required to eradicate erroneous opinion.[33] But if any magistrate were to become too free with his power as a result of this type of concession to necessity, he would be restrained by the pronouncements of the synod not only against the use of civil power to regulate essential ecclesiastical functions such as describing and restricting the form of church government, specifying membership qualifications, and directing intrachurch administration, but also by the synod's prohibition of the exercise of secular authority against those characterized as having erroneous opinions or who committed acts that were not clear violations of Scripture.

The effect of the *Cambridge Platform* as an anti-secular document was not apparent either to Mather or to his colleagues when it was completed in 1648 or when it was accepted by the General Court in 1651, but its importance became apparent in light of ensuing events in Massachusetts Bay. Although there was continuing interference in church functions after approval of the *Platform,* and a portion of it was at the behest of the clergy, the interference was limited to minor disputes.[33] On questions with far-ranging and profound religious implications, the Court's role was visibly altered by the new clerical sentiment for independence. It was no longer a body able to exercise powers of superintendency and arbitration but was relegated to a position of confused inadequacy. This was evident in the agonizing disagreements over eligibility for baptism. Here the General Court's relationship with the clergy represented a singular departure from the pre-1648 pattern. In contrast to the pivotal position it had taken on matters of church operation in earlier years, the secular power no longer dominated the debate, and the Court become instead a pawn in the ministerial confrontation between advocates and opponents of broadening eligibility for baptism.

The decline in the General Court's power to interfere in church affairs after 1651 would have been inconceivable in the years before the promulgation of the *Cambridge Platform,* and although there was a complex of causes, some local in nature and others directly related to events in England, for the decline in the General Court's dominance, Mather's "Modell of Church-Government" and the statement of faith derived from it are two of the most visible and influential of these. They were officially sanctioned statements of the direction being taken in the colony's second decade of settlement, and, more significantly, they indicated that Mather and at least some of his clerical and lay associates had departed from the traditional English pattern of church and state power relationships that they had brought with them across the Atlantic. But the strength of the ministerial opposition did not grow from unprepared soil. A large part of the independent clerical spirit that challenged the General Court had been planted and nurtured in the seed-bed of Richard Mather's frustration during his first years in America. The inclusion of Mather's ideological thrusts in the *Cambridge Platform* gave it the necessary form and structure to serve as the intellectual, legal, and theological underpinning for a clerical revolt that became a first step down the centuries-long path that would end only with complete separation of church and state.

Chapter Six

The Controversy Over Baptism

The problems surrounding baptism were complex and vexing issues for the residents of Massachusetts Bay during the first decades of settlement. The dispute over who could receive the sacrament was in part responsible for the summoning of the synod in 1646 and Richard Mather's unsuccessful attempt to provide a solution. But the question of eligibility that Mather had attempted to lay to rest was only one aspect of the colonists' disagreement. Less serious in its basic theological ramifications but equally aggravating was the failure of the Massachusetts Bay ministers to reach agreement on the correct ceremonial procedure for baptizing church members. Most clerics in the colony agreed that the ceremonial sprinkling of an infant was the divinely specified method of baptizing, but within the colony there were two factions that rejected the widely accepted ceremony. The first of these groups, led by clergyman Charles Chauncy, held that the correct form for baptism was to submerge the newborn child completely in water. A mere sprinkling, he argued, was inadequate. In 1642 he had done this with two of his own children in water so cold that one of them lost consciousness.[1] Despite his insistence on immersion, the practice was not generally accepted anywhere in New England. By itself, Chauncy's view presented no real threat to the widely accepted practice of administering baptism, but another facet of the problem was created by a segment of the community that opposed infant baptism entirely. No essential connection existed between the two rejections of standard Bay Colony baptismal practice, but there was at least some possibility for an alliance between those who rejected infant baptism and the advocates of complete immersion. Submerging an infant completely had obvious dangers, but if the subject of baptism were an adolescent, the drawbacks were eliminated. This was the pattern already successfully followed by Anabaptists in Europe, and if the two groups advocating deviant forms of baptism were to unite and then make common cause with those favoring presbyterial reforms in the colony's ecclesiastical structure, what had been merely an irritation could seriously widen the division already present over who was eligible to be baptized.

Refutation of John Spilsbury

The dissidents who denounced the generally accepted Massachusetts Bay baptismal ceremony were given encouragement in 1644 or 1645 with the arrival in the settlement of a work by John Spilsbury, an English Anabaptist.[2] In his book Spilsbury argued that only those children should be baptized who were old enough to understand the sacrament and accept or reject it of their own free will. The support such a doctrine could have given dissident elements represented a genuine threat in a colony already experiencing acute anxiety over almost every aspect of the nature of the first sacrament. The only course was to provide a refutation, and Mather, ever ready to defend Bay Colony faith and practice, undertook to produce a reply to Spilsbury. The product of his efforts was "An Answer to 9 Reasons of John Spilsbury to Prove Infants Ought Not to Be Baptized," a seventy-page point-by-point refutation.[3] Mather began by noting that few of Spilsbury's nine reasons offered any proof from Scripture of their validity (4), and he repeated this observation regularly, complaining angrily at one point that the reason offered "hath not so much as one word of God to confirme it, no nor not so much as any colour of consequence; but consisteth only of his owne bare word and naked affirmation, and that is all the proofe and strength that is in it: and therefore there is small reason for any to bee swayed thereby or to beleeve the same" (33).

Spilsbury not only neglected to shore up his reasons with citations, but he also refused to pay close heed to biblical events. He maintained in his first reason that infant baptism was unlawful because it was not used in the New Testament. Mather did not need to present a complex chain of reason or delve into the works of an agglomeration of theologians to counter the statement. He needed only to open his

Bible. Citing I Cor. 1: 16, "And I baptized also the household of
Stephanas," he insisted that the term *household* was inclusive of all
members, not limited to the adult residents(15). The same was also
true, he said, of Acts 16: 15, in reference to baptism of the household
of Lydia at Thyatira(15). Still, Mather's most persuasive rebuttal to
Spilsbury's first reason was that taken from Matthew 28: 19 where he
quoted Christ's injunction "Go ye therefore, and teach all nations,
baptizing them in the name of the Father, and of the Son, and of the
Holy Ghost." Here he insisted there could be no doubt(12). Christ
did not qualify his words nor did he equivocate. When he specified the
baptism of nations he did not caution his Apostles to baptize only the
adult population, he said baptize the nations. This could not be
construed in any way, Mather argued, except to include infants.
Mather continued his attack on Spilsbury's assertion that baptism of
infants was unlawful because it was not included in the New Testament
by employing typological arguments against the insistence that all
Christian practice must be drawn from examples since the time of
Christ. Using the familiar premise that circumcision in the Old
Testament was the justification for baptism in Christian churches, he
taunted Spilsbury, asking, "If nothing must be beleeved or practiced
without commandment or example and that from the new Testament
too, I would fayne know whether translations of the Scriptures from
the original Tongues into English [or using] such translations in
church-meetings is [illeg.] unlawfull for Christians"(9).
    Mather had no more problem with refuting any of the remaining
reasons than he had with the first. The techniques of scriptural citation
and typology that he had learned in earlier years were supplemented
by logic that he used with devastating effect on Spilsbury's assertions.
In the fourth reason against baptizing infants, the English cleric
insisted that the practice was prohibited because it made the recipient
unable to understand the ordinance when he reached maturity. Mather
seemed to take pleasure in answering Spilsbury's allegation of the
power of infant baptism to addle the mind sufficiently so that the true
nature and meaning of the sacrament could never be appreciated. He
replied with thinly veiled sarcasm, saying, "For who knowes not that
many baptised in Infancy have afterward understood the nature of
that ordinance, as well as if they had not received the same afore? I

suppose the Author of these reasons was himselfe baptised when he was an Infant, and so were many others who are now of his opinion and way. Now if this practise do keepe people in blindness that they can not come to know the nature of that holy ordinance, shall we then conclude that he and his fellowes are still holden in such blindness?'' (33-34). At another point, Mather became so perturbed at some of Spilsbury's arguments that he abandoned the calm line of discussion to denounce his opponent's case, noting in exasperation, "I may say . . . even the Lord that hath chosen Jerusalem rebuke thee, for two things in this reason are most grosse, and little better at the least the one of them, then blasphemous" (50). Mather did not encounter any abiding difficulties in refuting Spilsbury, and it was only the press of other duties rather than the Anabaptist's skill at argument that kept him from finishing the rebuttal before May, 1646.

It is unlikely that Mather intended his manuscript refutation of John Spilsbury's nine reasons against the baptizing of infants to be published in the colony where printing facilities were limited, nor was it likely that he planned to send the manuscript to London to be printed. While the subject was of interest to some in England, since nonconformists there were engaged in many of the same disagreements over baptism that divided the colonists, the dispute over infant baptism in a country where the triumph of presbyterial-style ecclesiastical polity seemed assured was not as serious as in Massachusetts where there was deep concern for the survival of the local religious order. Instead, Mather wrote to persuade his fellow settlers in the Bay of the correct method of administering the first sacrament, and as he wrote he was aware of the importance of what he did. He understood full well the dangers that could be created if the disputes raging over the nature of baptism were allowed to expand. John Spilsbury's book was the sort of work that had potential for further dividing and weakening a settlement that was already fearful of a confrontation with the presbyterian-dominated Parliament. Fortunately for the future of the Bay Colony's congregational pattern, Mather's tract was well received and probably aided in preventing the spread of antipaedobaptismal sentiment. The leaders of the movement, Charles Chauncy and several associates, were not persuaded of the error of their doctrine, but due at least in part to Mather's efforts, their method of administering the first sacrament did not gain adherents. They remained few in number, ideologically isolated, and were never able to make common cause with other dissidents and form part of any serious threat to the colony's ecclesiastical order.

The ease and self-assurance with which Mather dispatched John Spilsbury were deceptive. His refutation was positive, lucid, and definitive in tone, indicating a firm grip on all aspects of doctrine concerning baptism, but his clear and unvacillating appearance did not reflect the situation as it existed in the colony. The presbyterians, Anabaptists, and others who simply wanted wider eligibility for baptism were already having their effect on the colony's clerical leadership. In his *Church Government . . . an Answer to Two and Thirty Questions,* Mather had written, "Such Children whose Father and Mother were neither of them Believers, and sanctified, are counted by the Apostle (as it seemes to us) not faederally holy, but uncleane, what ever their other Ancestors have been . . . And therefore we Baptize them not."[4] By 1645, a year before the synod but when the obvious difficulties over limited eligibility for baptism were becoming apparent, his opinion began to change. This was clear enough in "A Plea for the Churches of Christ in New England," where his stand on baptism varied from section to section. At one point in the lengthy work he said that children were in the same state as their parents, implying that if parents were eligible for baptism, so were the children. At another place he obscured his meaning by adding that the right to baptism could not be transferred even by the grandparents. If it were possible to skip the biological parents' generation, he said, then baptism could be extended indefinitely, and by that means everyone would be qualified for church membership, or at least the degree of membership conferred by receiving the first sacrament. At still another place in the work, he was less certain. In reply to the rhetorical question "When those that were baptized in Infancy by the Covenant of their parents, being come to age are not yet found fitt to bee received to the Lords table, although they bee married and have children, whether are those their children to be baptized or no?"[5] he said, "It be not fitt to be peremptorie in a matter so dark and doubtful, yet til further light appear."[6] Then, after admitting that the course to be followed was not clear, he answered with a reply that was not consistent with what he had said elsewhere in the text. He stated that children of unregenerate but baptized parents should receive the sacrament if the parents led the sort of lives that were in concert with Christ's teaching.[7]

By the time of the synod of 1646 Mather was no longer unsure of the proper criteria for determining who should be entitled to baptism. In his "Modell of Church-Government," the draft statement of doctrine and polity he prepared for the synod, he attempted to persuade the clerical and secular representatives to accept the broadened eligiblity, but in the completed *Cambridge Platform* his suggestions were ignored and the synod affirmed the correctness of the previously accepted doctrine restricting baptism to the children of church members. Many who participated in the synod knew that disagreement on so vital a doctrine could not be easily ignored, and as they suspected, it was only a short time before the question came up again, but this time in a slightly altered context.

The newest difficulty began when John Cotton received a letter positing an unusual case. An unknown writer asked the Boston cleric what should be done when a baptized but unregenerate Christian died and left his infant to a church member who then adopted the orphan. Should the child be baptized? Cotton understood the ramifications in whatever answer he might give, and rather than act alone in so controversial a matter he posed the problem to John Eliot, John Wilson, and Richard Mather, asking them to give their opinions on the question. The selection of these three indicated that Cotton was not merely seeking advice but had made up his mind and simply hoped to get confirmation of his decision. While the precise opinions of Eliot are not clear on the subject of baptism, at least at this time, both Wilson and Mather were known to be supporters of widening eligibility to include children of baptized but unregenerate parents. As was expected, after examining the problem all three clerics returned affirmative answers to the question presented in the letter. This was a peculiar situation, differing in many respects from the central difficulty surrounding baptism, but the absence of any indecision let alone a negative answer on the part of all clerics confirmed that by 1648 there was genuine ministerial support for extending the definition of "seed" beyond the biological parent or parents.

Mather, Eliot, Wilson, and Cotton were not the only clerics in the colony who had moved away from the carefully described limits on administering the first sacrament by this time. As Cotton indicated by his choice of the three men, the fraternity of Massachusetts Bay clerics was in the process of doctrinal alteration. Sometime between 1646 and 1648, Mather became one of the most ardent advocates of making the change. He proselytized among his colleagues in the Bay Colony and other New England divines, discussing the difficulty and making known his opinions on the subject. Shortly before the adoption of the *Cambridge Platform,* Henry Smith of Wethersfield in Connecticut wrote to him asking advice and adding that his church favored baptizing the children of Christian but unregenerate parents. Mather's answering letter to Smith has not survived, but a short time later he wrote that he had openly favored broad baptism as early as 1646. Samuel Stone, another Connecticut cleric, wrote to the Dorchester church with the same problem in 1650, noting that both he and his fellow minister, John Warham, agreed that there was a need to make baptism more widely available. In his letter he mentioned the growing discontent among his congregants and suggested some sort of conference to deal with the difficulty. The following year, Peter Prudden, pastor at Milford in New Haven, lamented the division of opinion, feeling it aided those with presbyterian inclinations in their efforts to subvert congregationalism. He favored extending baptism to infant children of nonregenerate Christians as did Warham and Stone. Mather answered the letters he received and continued to write to other clerics championing wider admittance to the sacrament. He was successful in his efforts with at least one of his fellow clergymen. His letter to Nathaniel Rogers in 1652 probably induced Rogers to join the growing number of colonial clergy who supported a wider eligiblity for baptism.[8]

Intrachurch Government

Although Mather was active in pressing the cause of wider eligibility for baptism among his fellow ministers, he soon found that persuading his Dorchester church members of the divine sanction for his newly acquired view was much more difficult. The preacher first encountered resistance to expanded baptism from his parishioners in

1648 or 1650, and when this occurred, he found it a difficult thing to understand. The brethren had accepted his determinations on all theological questions in earlier years, and by every indication he was deeply admired not only by the church members but by all residents of the town. They had shown their estimation of his value year after year by granting him large amounts of land and by continually awarding him one of the largest clerical salaries in the colony. Although ministerial maintenance had repeatedly been a problem in various villages in the Bay and had received the regular attention of preachers of the stature of John Cotton and John Wilson, Mather had never experienced any difficulty on this account.[9] With an expression of respect and approval of this nature, it is certain that when he reflected on the reasons for the failure of the church to follow his lead on sacramental administration, Mather's own estimation of his abilities as well as the regular generosity of the townsmen undoubtedly caused him to rule out personal unpopularity as a reason. But in searching further, it is equally certain that he ignored the profound social implications inherent in a broadening of baptism, and instead he saw in the refusal to accept his new perception only the intransigence of many of his church members. As he had done when his new church was denied official sanction in 1636, he sought to lay the blame on the ordinary members, who had gained, much to his chagrin, a vital role in the governing of the church by the middle of the seventeenth century.

Distinction between cleric and brethren had always been emphasized by Mather in his writing and preaching, and over the years he regularly expressed an abiding distrust of the ordinary church member's judgment in ecclesiastical matters. When his church was denied official recognition during his first months in America, he wrote that the onus of failure lay with those prospective members who had given him advice on how to proceed, and since that time nothing had happened to alter his perception. It had been he, not the brethren, who had preserved the correct doctrine during the Antinomian crisis, shortly thereafter it was he who prevailed against a minor outbreak of separatist sentiment in Dorchester, and now, in 1650, it was he again who carried God's word on baptism.[10] It was clear to Mather that the brethren could not be trusted, and even though many of the colony's

ministers advocated a form of church government with power shared
by the elders and members, Mather had always thought otherwise. In
his sermons he expressed the need for harmony that could be had only
when the brethren submitted to the judgment of the eldership,[11] and
he repeated this in his writings. In *An Answer to Two Questions*, his
examination of the nature of the authority within individual churches,
he wrote, "Ministerial and delegated Government belongeth only to
the Elders. . . . So all are not Governours, but some only; and
therefore it cannot be that the Power of Church Government should
be in all the People. . . . The People are especially commanded to
Obey their Elders as their Rulers, and to submit themselves. . . .
Which plainly sheweth that the Power of Government and Rule is not
in the People at all, but in the Elders alone."[12] Although many of his
colleagues had attempted to soften this restrictive approach to church
government, holding that it was a mixed form "in respect of the
Elders, Aristocratical, and in respect of the People Democratical; and
therefore the People have some Share in the Government," Mather
remained suspicious of this approach, preferring the same system of
church government that was common in the diocese of Lancashire
when he had lived there years before. "They that so speak," he
answered, "do take Democracy in a large sense, to note that Liberty,
and Interest and Consent which the People have in Elections and
Censures, and the like: which tho' in Propriety of Speech, it be not
Government or Rule. . . . and . . . it may be granted, that Church
Government is not without some Democracy therein: Only heed must
be taken, that under a colour of a mixture . . . we do not Establish
. . . meer Democracy, and so destroy that mixture which we seem to
plead for. . . . The Elders must have at the least a Negative Voice, and
no matter pass Judicially without their Authoritative Concurrence in
the same" (17-18). Understandably, Mather made no mention of a
negative voice for the brethren, but by 1650, as a result of
congregational insistence on near unanimity in church matters, a
negative voice was exactly what the brethren had gained, and later, on
the matter of baptism, they used it with full effect to thwart Mather's
will.

This became apparent in the years after the adoption of the
Cambridge Platform when, although Mather was a recognized leader
in the movement to expand baptism and he regularly preached to his

flock on the scriptural justifications for doing so, he was unable to induce his church members even to discuss the matter. It was not until 1655, seven years after he first attempted to convince the synod to accept broadened eligibility, that he could persuade the Dorchester church to consider modifying their own restrictions on the availability of baptism. When the subject was ultimately introduced for debate, any members desiring to speak were allowed to state their views. The discussion indicated that Mather was correct in discerning some support for baptizing the children of parents who were baptized but never fully admitted to the church, but even at this time the brethren's distrust of their minister on the issue was made apparent when, unwilling to accept his word on so weighty a matter, they requested the opinions of the churches in four neighboring villages. The answers they received were little comfort to men who desired guidance, for the three churches that replied were as divided on the question as was Dorchester. Rather than accept Mather's determination without further doctrinal buttressing, the church made no decision, thereby rejecting implicitly their minister's advocacy of broader baptism and retaining their practice of baptizing only the children of church members.[13]

A Disputation Concerning Church-Members and Their Children

While Mather and his church debated on the proper manner of administering the first sacrament, a series of events was taking place that though only partially connected with baptism would bring the colonial ecclesiastics to the point where they would have to confront directly the question of eligibility for the first sacrament. Between the years 1653 and 1659, a bitter quarrel raged in Hartford over the selection of a cleric to replace the deceased Thomas Hooker. The disruption brought about by the disagreements emboldened a few nonmembers of the church, and they petitioned the General Court of Connecticut, asking for a relaxation of the restrictions surrounding baptism. The Connecticut governing body deputized a committee to examine the petitioners' request, and, to aid in making a decision, the opinion of the Massachusetts Bay General Court was sought in the summer of 1656.

The autumn following the inquiry, the Massachusetts Court,

realizing the true extent of the problem, called for a meeting of the colonies to discuss the points at issue. Some idea of the gravity legislators attached to the meeting was indicated when they ordered Robert Turner, a Boston innkeeper, to "provide convenient entertaynment for the said gentlemen during their attendance on the said meeting" with the cost to be borne by the colony.[14] The ministers from Massachusetts and Connecticut, some twenty in all, convened in June, 1657. Mather's account of the debates, *A Disputation Concerning Church-Members and Their Children,* revealed that it took the conference nineteen days of discussion before they agreed to sanction what would be called the half-way covenant, the extension of baptism to the children of those parents who were baptized but not admitted as full church members.[15] While there were a number of clerics at the meeting whose opinions "met not with the rest," Mather was with those who stood with the majority. The decision of the clergymen on this vital issue strengthened Mather's position in dealing with his own church. He now had the combined authority of the Connecticut and Massachusetts Bay ministry behind him, and he was to need it, for, soon after the meeting ended, his Dorchester church was directly confronted with the problem when the newborn granddaughter of one of the church elders was presented for baptism by her baptized but unregenerate father.

This represented a perfect opportunity for Mather to explain more clearly to his church the need for broadened baptism. By this time he had already completed his *Disputation Concerning Church-Members and Their Children* and now he had the opportunity to offer the arguments to his church. Mather knew that on so divisive an issue he would have to structure his presentation carefully to assure that it would be understood even by the dullest member of the company. He began with the initial premise used by most of his colleagues when they argued for broader baptism. "Some Children of confederate Parents," he asserted confidently, "are by meanes of their Parents Covenanting, in Covenant also, and so Members of the Church by divine Institution" (1). Such a statement, while easy enough to make, was especially difficult to establish as fact, but it was necessary to do so, for without it Mather's case would crumble. He began his defense of the premise by insisting that the covenant established in the Old

Testament was surely applicable to the seventeenth century. He patiently explained "some children are in that Covenant for substance which was made with Abraham . . . as appears by sundry Scriptures, which being rightly considered, and compared, do inferre the continuance of the substance of that Covenant, whereby God is a God to his People and their seed, under the New Testament" (2). He confirmed this with a torrent of examples from the Old Testament, from the life of Christ, and with a host of citations ranging from Genesis almost to Revelation. (2-3).

As he moved from example to example and from premise to premise, there were repeated demands from the brethren to clarify minor points on which confusion had already arisen. What of children of various ages; were they in covenant as were their parents? What of children never brought to the church? What of children born before their parents' convenanting? What of incorrigibles of seven, or eight, or twelve years old or of children who did not desire to be associated with the church? These minor issues were often difficult and troublesome for Mather. They took time, patient and involved explanation, and served to divert attention from the argument he was attempting to construct, but before he could complete the line of logic, he was forced to answer such queries. Only then could he bring the debate back to the central issue, the question of "Whether the child admitted by his Fathers Covenant, be also a Deputy for his seed, without or before personal Covenanting, or without and before like personal qualifications in kind, as his Father was to enjoy when he became a Deputy" (20). Mather retreated continually to his opening premise to provide unequivocal proof for this statement. He insisted that "Infants either of whose immediate Parents are in Church-Covenant, do confæderate with their Parents, and are therefore Church-members with them" (20). These children, then, "In case they understand the grounds of Religion, are not scandalous, and solemnly own the Covenant in their own persons, wherein they give up both themselves and their children unto the Lord, and desire Baptism for them, we (with due reverence to any Godly Learned that may dissent) see not sufficient cause to deny Baptism unto their children" (21). This last statement, diffidently offered with a provision to avoid giving offense to the opposition brethren, was supported by half a dozen arguments and reasons. "Church-Members without offence and not baptized," Mather explained, "are to be baptized." He then added more premises and deductions in quick succession to support his logic. "Children in the covenant of Abraham, as to the substance thereof . . . are to be baptized. The children in Question are children in the covenant of Abraham. . . . Therefore the children in Question are to be baptized." "Children in the same estate with those children under the Law . . . are to be baptized. . . . the children in Question are in the same estate . . . with those children under the Law. . . . Therefore the children in Question are to be baptized" (21-22).

After the syllogisms, Mather closed with an attempt to assuage fears that the sanctuary would be corrupted by the admission of a host of unworthies. "Though the persons forementioned own the Covenant according to the premises," he assured his listeners, "yet before they are admitted to full communion . . . they must so hold forth their Faith and Repentance, unto the judgment of Charity by way of confession in the congregation, as it may appear unto the Church, that they are able to examine themselves and to discern the Lord's body" (24). Even with all his reasoning, examples, citations, and exhortation, Mather was not sufficiently convincing. The Dorchester church refused to assent to the desire of their teacher and baptism was denied to the infant.[16]

Mather was deeply discouraged by the division within his church over the attempt to have the child baptized, and not until three years had passed did he see another opportunity to persuade his Dorchester saints to follow his lead and accept broader eligibility for baptism. In May, 1660, he again brought the matter before his church. After an evening service he told the members he wished to speak on an important matter. He informed them that he had conferred earlier with the other elders of the church and they agreed with what he was about to say. Then he explained to those assembled, as he had explained on previous occasions:

"Such children as are [the seed of church members] affirmed to have a place and portion in the Kingdome of Heaven, they have a place and portion in the visible Church, and so consequently are members thereof. . . . If children were once Church-members and do not continue to be Church-members still, then their Membership must have been repealed by the Lord, who alone could make such an alteration: And if any should affirm that the Lord hath done it, it lieth upon them to prove it. (3,11)

It followed from this, he maintained, using the same arguments he had embodied in the *Disputation Concerning Church-Members and Their Children,* that though some children of members had yet to be admitted to the privilege of voting and to the Lord's table, still they were members, they should be treated as such, and their children should be baptized.[17]

There were no immediate repercussions from Mather's announcement, but it was only a matter of months before the church was again in the midst of another confrontation. It began in the autumn of 1660, when the teacher once more asked the membership to remain after the conclusion of services. He then informed them that the wife of James Minot had requested baptism for her children. Neither of the Minots were full members of the Dorchester church though both had been baptized under their parents' covenants. Those present discussed the matter but reached no conclusion. The following week the subject was broached again, but the opposition to the opinion of the minister was strong, and once more they failed to reach agreement. After letting the matter rest for several weeks, the church leadership decided to press for a decision. Elder Henry Withington rose, stood before the entire congregation, and said he had discussed Mather's proposal to baptize children with members of the church over the past several days and found that many wanted more debate on the problem.[18] One by one Mather's now-familiar arguments were presented. Opponents of expanding sacramental administration argued that the children of baptized parents who were not members in full communion were deficient in glory, mercy, and other blessings, and should be denied the sacrament. Others in agreement with them added that though the parents were church members, the child should be denied baptism because the parents were not members in the truest sense of the term. Mather again returned to the *Disputation Concerning Church-Members and Their Children* to counter these lines of reasoning, saying, "The Church-act onely, and not any other act (much lesse defect) of the Parent is by Divine Institution, accounted to the child. The

membership of the child is a distinct membership, from the membership of the Parent. In case the Parents membership ceaseth by death
or censure, the membership of the child remaineth still. . . . The child
is baptized by vertue of his own membership, and not by vertue of his
Parents membership" (23-24). This was not sufficient to move the
members, nor were any of Mather's other arguments, and again no
decision was reached. After this discussion, the intensity of the debate
made it clear that nothing approaching unanimity could be achieved,
and the question of eligibility for baptism was dropped.[19]

The Synod of 1662

The Dorchester disagreement over who should receive the first
sacrament was soon complicated by events on the opposite side of the
Atlantic. With the death of Oliver Cromwell, the passing of the
Protectorate, and the restoration of Charles II, the future of the
colonial churches and governments was uncertain. Even though the
new king made many promises not to attempt an expansion of his
authority, there was much doubt about a Stuart on the throne. In
response to the continuing uncertainty, Mather's church proclaimed a
series of fasts. Often they were brought about by some difficulty in the
colony, but in almost every case the failure of the nonconformists in
England to establish a viable government and the return of the king
and the Anglican Church were included as reasons for their procla-
mation. Usually the fasts were local, proclaimed by the authority of
the church, but in May, 1662, concern in the colony grew so great
that the General Court announced that a day would be set aside for
fasting and prayer because of sickness in the colony and the adverse
events in England.[20]

With the situation in the homeland growing more unfavorable as
time passed, the Bay Colonists knew that they must have uniformity at
home, but the meeting on baptism in 1657, while it had endorsed
half-way covenanting, had not settled the question to the satisfaction
of enough settlers to insure that there would be no serious disagreements. There was also the agonizing theological problem created by
the very presence of divergent views on baptism. There had never been
any attempt in the colony to insure absolute ceremonial uniformity
among the churches. Deviations on minor points were tolerated in

New England, but with something as important as baptism, disagreement could not be permitted indefinitely. There was only one way prescribed by God, and it had to be discovered for the benefit of all. A meeting was needed to settle the problem permanently.

The synod appointed to resolve the differences over the first sacrament was scheduled to convene on the second Tuesday of March, 1662. Approximately a fortnight before the meeting was to begin, the Dorchester church received official notification that they were to send representatives to Boston for the deliberations. The two men chosen to speak for the church were the minister and his youngest son, Increase. On the appointed day in March, the father and son gathered with representatives of the other churches of Massachusetts Bay at the meetinghouse of the First Church in Boston. In all, some seventy men came to the conference to test arguments and to extract a solution from the theological interplay. The assembly was divided into two camps from the beginning, those who supported the solution put forth by the 1657 meeting of ministers and those who opposed it. The clerics who favored restricted baptism numbered a few more than ten, while the remainder favored enlargement of the number eligible. Among those who composed the smaller faction were Charles Chauncy, by this time the President of Harvard, John Mayo of the Second Church in Boston, and two of Richard Mather's sons, Increase and Elazer, the minister to the church at Northampton. Mather himself was numbered with the advocates of extended baptism.[21]

The synod lasted until autumn, although it did not meet continuously for the six months it was in session. The clerics conferred in three relatively abbreviated conferences during the spring and summer before they made a decision. On September 27, the Dorchester church was notified that agreement had been reached. The majority, those who favored baptizing the children of Christian but unregenerate parents, carried the day. Still, in spite of their victory, they failed to convince the minority of their errors, and so their view did not prevail with unanimity.

A Defense of the Answer and Arguments of the Synod

The vanquished ministers in the synod were outvoted by a substantial margin but they were not in retreat. They were numerous

enough and sufficiently confident in the rectitude of their beliefs so
that they could not be compelled to accept their minority position as
an indication of defeat. Despite being outnumbered, they remained a
cohesive and articulate segment of the colony's ecclesiastical community. Having failed to persuade their clerical colleagues of the divine
sanctions for restrictive baptism, they tried a new tactic. They sought
to gain support for their cause by appealing to the traditionalism of the
colony's settlers. This was particularly evident in the pamphlet battle
over the half-way covenant that followed the dissolution of the synod.
As soon as the participants in the conclave returned to their homes the
debate began. Charles Chauncy produced his *Anti-Synodalia Scripta
Americana* to express the minority view, and he was answered by John
Allin, the minister of Dedham, who spoke for the majority. Increase
was the first of the Mathers into the fray. He wrote an unsigned
preface to John Davenport's book arguing against the decision of the
synod. A reply to the work of young Mather and Davenport was
composed by Jonathan Mitchel, the guiding force of the majority party
in the synod, and Richard Mather. The two men divided the answer
between them. Mitchel wrote the rebuttal to Increase Mather's
anonymous preface, and the senior Mather attempted to refute
Davenport. Their joint effort was published under a single title as *A
Defense of the Answer and Arguments of the Synod.*[22]

The battle waged by Davenport, Chauncy, Mitchel, the Mathers,
and others who joined in the exchange was far different in direction
than the earlier polemical confrontations fought only among the
members of the ministry. In the disputes of previous years, the lines of
division were largely within the clergy, and all sides endeavored to
limit the extent of disagreement to those who were conversant with
the intricacies of theology, doctrine, and polity. In 1662 the caution of
past confrontations was abandoned, and the synod's minority, realizing
they could go no further in trying to prevail among the clerical
community, attempted to regain what they had lost by turning the
colony's ordinary church members against the ministerial majority
who favored the half-way solution. The new tactic was particularly
evident to supporters of the synod's recommendations like Mitchel
who wrote to one of the dissenters "For the People in the Country
have in a manner no Arguments to object but this, some of yourselves,

some of the Ministers are against it." [23] In his *Another Essay for the Investigation of Truth* John Davenport tried to deny the nature of the anti-synodalian arguments by insisting that he was only seeking "Truth with Peace," but the inaccuracy of his assertion was apparent in Increase Mather's preface to the same work. The younger Mather admitted the purpose of the book was to gain as wide an audience for the anti-synodalian argument as possible. He said, "We are willing that the World should see what is here presented. But especially, being perswaded that the Honour of God, and of his Truth, require this as a duty at our hands, We durst not hinder what is here maintained from coming into light, lest we should one day have it laid unto our Charge, that we did withhold the Truth in unrighteousness." [24]

Unlike both his son Increase and John Davenport, Richard Mather did not comprehend the true nature of the polemical battle over the synod's decision. In his defense, he stayed close to the issues, rarely allowing his arguments to drift into denunciation or mere rhetoric. As he explained, his reply to Davenport was not to be a restatement of the propositions adopted in 1662. He sought only to refute the work of one man, and this he did in the tightly compartmented style he had used in his first defense of the Bay Colony's religion three decades before. In premise after premise and deduction after deduction he offered scriptural citation, the work of scholars ranging from the days of the primitive church to the time of John Cotton, and his own logic to defend the half-way covenant. By 1662 the task at hand was to persuade the ordinary church members of the need and divine sanction for expanding the number eligible for baptism rather than to convince one theologian of the error of his ways, but Mather never understood this.

His failure to communicate his position on baptism was nowhere more clearly illustrated than in his own village church when, shortly after the closing of the synod, there was another confrontation over who could receive the first sacrament. It began when Mrs. Israel Stoughton, the town's leading matron, and her daughter, Rebecca Taylor, requested that the Taylor children be allowed to receive baptism, even though the mother was a member of the church only through the covenant of her parents. The minister, whose hearing was failing noticeably and who was now sightless in one eye, could not have been cheered by the bitterness the request generated, and he attempted to avoid a direct clash of factions similar to that of some years earlier when one of the church elders had requested baptism for his granddaughter even though his son and daughter-in-law had not been admitted as full members to the Dorchester church.[25] At the request of the elders and brethren Mather conferred with the mother to try and find if she would join in full communion with the church and thereby remove the impediment to her children's baptism. On October 24, 1668, he reported that the conference with the woman was not successful. Mrs. Taylor told him "she did not Judge her self worthy or as yet fitt for the lords supp, and therefore durst not adventure ther uppon but yet did desier baptizme for her Children."[26] The question was then debated again, but neither side would relent. Consensus was not to be gained, and Dorchester was prevented from taking any action. They retained their restrictions on sacramental administration, and the children were not baptized. This was Mather's last attempt to get his church to accept the results of the determinations of 1657 and 1662, and he failed. His disappointment at the rebuke from those he had served so long was a painful thing to the aged minister, even more painful, perhaps, than his rejection years before by the First Church in Boston and the General Court. Long the champion of expanded baptism, he had been one of the guiding spirits in the battle for its acceptance. Then, after it received approval by most of the colony's leading ecclesiastical figures, some of the local churches, and was widely accepted in Connecticut, he remained unable to persuade his own membership to follow his lead.

The failure of the Dorchester church to adopt broader eligibility for baptism, his diminishing vigor, and the death of John Wilson, the minister to the First Church in Boston, were all part of a series of events that saddened Mather in the years after the 1662 synod. One after another, the men with whom he had worked and endeavored to build a land according to the revealed will of God were dying. Winthrop had passed away in 1649 and Hooker shortly before. Gone, too, were Cotton, Thomas Shepard, and Peter Bulkley. John Norton, his friend and confidant, was another who had joined the host of founders in death. Mather was especially grieved by Norton's passing, and at his funeral "Wept over him . . . a Sermon most agreeable to the occasion."[27] To make his mood even more gloomy, in 1668 Mather was asked to participate in the adjudication of yet another controversy over baptism. The dispute began when the First Church in Boston called John Davenport of New Haven to fill the vacancy created by John Wilson's death. A minority within the church opposed his selection, objecting to his advanced age and his continued opposition to the half-way covenant. Under Wilson, the Bostonians had accepted broadened eligibility for baptism, but Davenport was determined to return the church to its earlier regulations. A further complication was that the minority opposed to Davenport were agitating for permission to leave the First Church and form their own religious body.[28]

In August, 1668, the church at Dorchester received an invitation from Boston asking them to send representatives to advise on Davenport's appointment. They complied with the request, and a delegation headed by Mather made the trip to Boston. There they met with representatives of other churches from August 6 to 8. Three days later Mather reported the results of the conference to his own church. He told them the Bostonians were advised to call Davenport as their pastor and to allow the dissident members to depart and gather their own church. The recommendations were accepted in part, and Davenport and his family were admitted to membership in November. The next month he was ordained pastor of the church.[29]

The second part of the recommendations made by the August meeting was not followed. When Davenport became pastor, he joined the majority party in refusing to allow the dissenters to depart and gather their own church. The dissident faction, thwarted by the new minister, made another attempt to gain dismission. They sent a call for the elders to convene again at Boston, reexamine the case, and make a new recommendation. Mather's health had been deteriorating over the months preceding the call for the meeting, but he was still able to serve as a member of the Dorchester delegation sent to advise the Bostonians. The conference began on April 13, 1669, and because of his "Age, Gravity, Grace, and Wisdom," Mather was chosen as moderator. After three days of deliberation the assembly adjourned after recommending once more the dismission of the dissenting brethren.[30]

On the final day of the conclave, Mather became ill, and in extreme discomfort due to total stoppage of urine, the septuagenarian was moved by coach from Boston to his home in Dorchester. Mather had experienced difficulties with kidney stones on previous occasions, but this time the problem was more serious. The pain continued to grow in intensity, but the only indication of his agony was an occasional groan he could not suppress. On the morning of April 22 he asked friends to help him to his study, for he had neglected his work for several days. They did as he requested, but even with their aid he could not get from his chamber. The pain continued and later in the day his voice deserted him.[31] That night "he quietly breathed forth his last; after he had been about Seventy-Three Years a Citizen of the World, and Fifty Years a minister in the Church of God."[32]

Chapter Seven
Conclusion

Richard Mather, like all of Massachusetts Bay's early writers, was raised in England and educated by men who demanded ecclesiastical reform and spirited resistance to authority. When opposition to the reformers grew strong during the reign of Charles I, many of them migrated to Massachusetts Bay. After they arrived in New England and assumed charge of village churches in the colony, they abandoned the anti-authoritarian character that had been a vital element in their movement and they began to write and preach a message that called for order, stability, and obedience to government. Their freshly acquired conservative bent was a natural outgrowth of the position of leadership they filled within their fledgling churches. In demanding reform while in the mother country, the immigrant clerics opposed an extant and functioning ecclesiastical system, but in the Bay their position was diametrically reversed. They no longer labored to cleanse and simplify a church along the lines they saw commanded by Scripture. Instead, they worked to discover a practical means for building true churches of Christ in America and perpetuating them once they had been completed. The result was that in the first half-decade of settlement, the literature of the Bay Colony was concerned primarily with day-to-day matters of polity and doctrine rather than with theory and it was designed to protect and preserve the local churches rather than to innovate.

Mather entered this ecclesiastically conservative community in 1635, and except for some initial difficulty, he fitted in well with the intellectual tenor of his new home for over ten years. He accepted the distinctions that separated New England religion from the nonconformity practiced in his native Lancashire, and he wrote and preached extensively in defense of Massachusetts Bay's faith. Nonconformist debate and writing over the preceding three quarters of a century set the patterns for ecclesiastical disputation in the Bay, and in his works explaining and substantiating religion in the colony, Mather offered no innovations in style or content. When he sent his description of colonial religion to E.B. in 1636, or when he answered the group of Lancashire clerics and Richard Bernard three years later, he wrote in a terse technical style that closely followed the questions he endeavored to answer or the objections he attempted to rebut. It was not until the 1640s that Mather moved away from the narrow didacticism common to nonconformist works. The first example of his deviation came in the *Answer to Mr. Herle,* where exasperation with Herle's ineptitude was expressed in frequent innuendo and sarcastic asides. Whether Mather's new approach was the result of his collaboration with William Tompson or simply irritation over the book cannot be determined, but it is clear that the revised style later served him well in venting rage and frustration against William Rathband, who used the letter to E.B., *Church Government . . . an Answer to Two and Thirty Questions,* and *An Apologie* so disingenuously in his account of church practices in New England. Mather's departure from the stylistic constraints of nonconformity was first confined to attacks against the colony's clerical detractors on the opposite side of the Atlantic, but it was only a short time before he employed his new techniques on the secular leadership of the Bay Colony. In the draft platform of church government presented to the synod in 1648, he incorporated the disputatious tone of the replies to Herle and Rathband with a large measure of bitter invective and found the mixture worked well. Even though the vituperation was edited out of his draft before its publication as the *Cambridge Platform,* Mather's presentation gained the synod's approval for the substance of his anti-magisterial reforms, and the methods he used could not be ignored by his colleagues.

After secular control over the churches declined following the acceptance of the *Platform,* the clergy soon discovered the only alternative source of support available to them was the church members of the colony. In a short time they found Mather's angry and aggressive rhetoric was more effective in gaining public support than the older style of disputation, and in later disagreements over baptism they abandoned writing technical treatises useful only for influencing clerics and began to employ the Dorchester cleric's techniques to popularize their arguments in hope of gaining the allegiance of the brethren. The effect of the new argumentative style was nowhere more apparent than in Mather's own failure to persuade his church to accept the half-way covenant. In the discussions he held with the Dorchester brethren and in his *Defense of the Answer and Arguments of the Synod,* Mather avoided the heated disputatious tone he had used in earlier years. He was not dealing with faraway Englishmen whose feelings and sensibilities could be ignored nor was he raging against the expanded powers of the General Court when he fought for the half-way covenant. In arguing to support the widening of eligibility for baptism, he opposed clerical colleagues with whom he had been closely associated for decades, men who could not be insulted, derided, or treated as inferiors. Throughout the debates with the church members and in his defense of the synod, Mather argued as a theologian argues, with carefully wrought logic, copious references to authority, and frequent scriptural citation. As a result, while his presentments were accepted by a preponderant majority of the colony's clergy who agreed that the first sacrament could be given to the children of baptized but unregenerate parents without violating the commands of God, he was unable to persuade his own church that this was true. In contrast, the opponents of the synod, with their flagrant appeal to the colony's church members were much more successful than Mather in gaining lay adherents to their position. Throughout the colony, in church after church, hostility to the half-way covenant grew so great that decades passed before substantial numbers of Massachusetts Bay villages could be persuaded to adopt the policy recommended by the synod.

The durability of the vituperative style and anti-secular tone popularized by Mather was nowhere more evident than in the election sermons preached in the years when the controversy over the half-way covenant was nearing its height. Jonathan Mitchel, Mather's literary collaborator in the campaign to widen eligibility for the first sacrament, abandoned any pretense of clerical humility or reserve when he preached a 1667 sermon informing the legislators that they must remember their place and keep to it. "The people are not for the Rulers," he said, "but the Rulers for the people.... and the more aptly and fully that any do serve to their End, the better and more excellent they are." Then, continuing with words chosen to appeal to an enlarged audience—but hardly selected to sway the minds of men trained in theology—he added that even in Nehemiah's time "there were faults, evils . . . sinful Corruptions and Distempers . . . among a Reforming people," and, he assured his listeners, God would not smite a people who were in the process of reform, for what was transpiring in the colony was true reformation.[1] Not to be outdone, William Stoughton, who opposed Mather on the issue of the half-way covenant, had no reservations about using his rhetorical style the following year in a lengthy sermon in which he called for a return to the faith of the colony's founders. He warned the Court that "There is no Errour in Doctrine, or in Worship and Ordinances, but it tends some way or other to alter, pervert, and corrupt the Lords Covenant with his people. By this we are to judge of the danger of Errours and erroneous practices, and answerably to watch against the infection of them."[2] Even John Davenport, the aged and revered patriarch of New England, abandoned the habits of moderation he had cultivated for decades and launched a bitter attack on the General Court in his election sermon of 1669, charging that interference in church matters was an abuse of their power and warning them that "People so give Magistratical Power unto some, as that still they retain in themselves these Three Acts, 1. That they may measure out so much Civil Power, as God in his Word alloweth to them. . . . 2. That they may set bounds and banks to the exercise of that Power. . . . 3. That they give it out conditionally . . . so as, if the condition be violated, they may resume their power of chusing another. . . . Take heed and beware that you deprive not any Instituted Christian Church . . . of the Power and Priviledges which Christ hath purchased for them by his precious blood."[3]

The dispute over baptism grew in intensity in the months after Davenport preached to the brethren against the Court, and the oratorical and literary efforts of the clergy to involve the colony's ordinary residents were so successful that the debate over the issues soon involved almost every church member in the Bay. The heat generated by the controversy was well illustrated by the actions of the deputies, most of whom were advocates of the anti-synodalian faction. Piqued by the refusal of the assistants to join them and incensed over the clerical majority's position in opposition to their own, they vented their rage in a blast of anti-clericalism unparalleled in the colony's history. The ministers were accused by a majority of the deputies of "declension from the primitive foundation worke, innovation in doctrine and worship, opinion and practice, and invasion of the rights, liberties, and priviledges of churches . . . and all this with a dangerous tendencie to the utter devastation of these churches, turning the pleasant gardens of Christ into a wilderness . . . that these are the leven, the corrupting gangreens, the infecting spreading plague . . . the chief incendaries of wrath and procurers of judgment on the land."[4]

Bay clerics had never before been attacked with such vehemence, but with their new mood of hostility toward secular authority and their weapons of pulpit and press honed to a fine edge, they were ready to repel the assault. Although Mather was dead over a year by the time of the confrontation between clerics and deputies, the ministers involved in the dispute responded with a flurry of unprecedented activity designed to defeat at the next election those deputies who supported the anti-clerical manifesto. The details of the ministerial campaign are obscure, but it is apparent that, throughout the winter of 1670 and in the spring of 1671, they wrote and preached continuously to persuade their parishioners to elect men sympathetic to them. The campaign was successful, and in May the clerical candidates won an overwhelming victory. The effect of the techniques of persuasion and denunciation was easily visible from the election results. In earlier years, the makeup of the lower house changed slowly, but after the election of 1671 a new majority was in command. Clerically supported deputies outnumbered the opposition by a margin of four to three. The election had so aroused passions that thirteen towns changed their representation entirely, and enough of the towns that in the past neglected to send any representatives now realized the need to do so, enlarging the house by one third. Almost half a dozen towns increased the size of their delegations from one to two representatives.[5]

When the General Court reconvened, the clergy, greatly buoyed by their electoral triumph, presented a reply to the charges levied by the previous lower house. The expected rebuttal was graciously accepted by the new members, and although those deputies still in the legislature who had the year before voted to condemn the clergy insisted that their negative votes on the recantation be counted, this did not veil the fact that the ministers had challenged the civil power with an appeal to the people of the Massachusetts Bay Colony and won a singular victory. Confirmation of this was not long in coming. Shortly thereafter, Thomas Shepard, Jr., while lamenting the deterioration of the cooperative spirit between leaders of church and state, publicly denounced the previous attempts of the magistracy to control the clergy, saying that while it was necessary for the civil government to exert power as they had done against various heretics in the past, this power could become dangerous when men failed to distinguish between the magistrates coercive power and abuse of that power in matters of religion.[6] In the next year's election sermon Urian Oakes repeated the same restrictions on the General Court. He informed them that "it is the duty of the Civil Magistrate to tolerate what is tolerable, and that some Errors are tolerable, as to the practice of them. For the Conscience [of] our persuasion about them is not immediately under the Magistrates Cognizance."[7]

The oratorical and literary style designed to reach a wide audience became popular in the later years of the seventeenth century and in the eighteenth century because it was well suited to the needs of the times. But in the 1640s Mather's opposition to the government and his use of spirited rhetoric represented genuine innovation, for even though his rhetorical style was only a resurrection of the anti-establishment devices used by nonconformists in the days of Elizabeth and James I, they were techniques that had been lost or forgotten in conservative Massachusetts Bay. The methods he used in replying to Herle, Rutherford, Rathband and in his attack on secular power in the "Modell of Church-Government" became a regular part of clerical preaching and writing. They were used in the dispute over baptism after 1662, in the ousting of Governor Edmund Andros at the time of the Glorious Revolution, in the disagreements over Stoddardism that plagued the colony in the closing years of the seventeenth century, throughout the fight for control of Harvard College, and in the Great Awakening decades later. Still, the most visible evidence of the lasting effect of Richard Mather's hostility to civil authority and his rhetorical innovations did not come until over one hundred years after his death when clergymen everywhere in New England used his methods from the pulpit and in print to denounce the government of George III and build support for the war that would create the United States of America.

Notes and References

Chapter One

1. William F. Irvine, "Parents of Reverend Richard Mather," *New England Historical and Genealogical Register* 54 (1900):348-49.

2. Increase Mather, *The Life and Death of that Reverend Man of God, Mr. Richard Mather, Teacher of the Church in Dorchester in New England* (Cambridge, Mass. Bay, 1670), p. 3.

3. Kenneth Murdock, *Increase Mather: The Foremost American Puritan* (Cambridge, Mass., 1925), p. 2; Increase Mather, *Life of Richard Mather*, pp. 3-4.

4. Increase Mather, *Life of Richard Mather*, pp. 3-5.

5. Ibid., pp. 5-6; see also Anthony à Wood, *Athenae Oxonienses*, 3d ed. (London, 1817), III, 832.

6. Increase Mather, *Life of Richard Mather*, pp. 6, 7.

7. Ibid., p. 7.

8. Ibid.; Cotton Mather gave the date as November 13, 1618, in his *Magnalia Christi Americana* (London, 1702), III, 124.

9. Increase Mather, *Life of Richard Mather*, p. 8; W. J. Lowenberg, ed., *The Registers of the Parish Church of Bury in the County of Lancaster* (Rochdale, Eng., 1898), p. 356.

10. Increase Mather, *Life of Richard Mather*, p. 8; Horace E. Mather, *The Lineage of Rev. Richard Mather* (Hartford, 1890), p. 33.

11. J.A. Picton, ed., *Selections from the Municipal Archives and Records of Liverpool from the 13th to the 17th Century Inclusive* (Liverpool, 1883), I, p. 200.

12. Thomas Hutchinson, *The Hutchinson Papers* (Albany, N.Y.: The Prince Society, 1865), p. 271; Increase Mather, *Life of Richard Mather*, p. 10; "Court Book" (Diocese of Chester), R.VI.A.23, 2, Borthwick Institute, York, Eng., pp. 316, 376.

13. Increase Mather, *Life of Richard Mather*, p. 11.

14. Ibid., p. 20; "Letter of John Cotton to a Puritan Minister in England, December 3, 1634," original in the Hutchinson MSS., Massachusetts Historical Society, Boston, Mass. Printed in Alexander Young, *Chronicles of the First Planters of the Colony of Massachusetts Bay, From 1623 to 1636* (New York, 1846), pp. 438-44.

15. The letters from Cotton and Hooker were not Mather's first contact with the network for dissemination of nonconformist propaganda that functioned in England during the reigns of Elizabeth, James I, and Charles I. Shortly before his difficulties with the hierarchy he acquired at least two letters written by Cotton which he thought were important enough to copy before passing them on. One dealt with the time of day when the sabbath began, the other, concerning separatism, was addressed to Samuel Skelton in New England. The copies are among the Richard Mather MSS. at the American Antiquarian Society, Worcester, Mass. By 1632, Mather obtained at least one other nonconformist tract, and as he had done with the letters by Cotton, he made his own copy. The document, with a heading of "5 Questions Answered," was a tirade against the wearing of vestments. Richard Mather MS., Gratz Collection, No. 8-23, The Historical Society of Pennsylvania, Philadelphia, Pa.

16. Increase Mather, *Life of Richard Mather*, pp. 17, 19; The manuscript of the reasons was first printed in 1670, a year after Mather's death. Ibid., pp. 12-19.

17. Young, *Chronicles*, pp. 438-44.

18. John Foxe, *The Acts and Monuments of John Foxe* (London, 1563), VII, 328, 497. Another staple of Mather's reading at this time was John Brinsley's *The True Watch* (London, 1622), a catalog of persecutions visited on Protestants.

19. Foxe, *Acts and Monuments*, VII, 194.

20. Richard Mather, *Journal of Richard Mather, 1635*, in *Collections of the Dorchester Antiquarian and Historical Society*, No. 3 (Boston, 1850).

21. Increase Mather, *Life of Richard Mather*, p. 20.

22. Richard Mather, *Journal*, pp. 26-29; John Winthrop, *Journal History of New England*, in *Original Narratives of Early American History*, ed. James K. Hosmer (New York, 1908), I, 155-57.

23. Richard Mather, *Journal*, p. 29. The portions of the *Journal* written after the landing in Boston have not survived.

Chapter Two

1. Young, *Chronicles*, p. 427.

2. The terms *congregational, congregationalist, presbyterial*, and *presbyterian* are not used in the hard denominational sense, but instead refer only to systems of polity or church government.

3. Larzer Ziff, *The Career of John Cotton: Puritanism and the American Experience* (Princeton, N.J., 1962), p. 49.

4. Ibid. pp. 71-105; Cotton Mather, *Magnalia*, III, 20-21.

5. Richard Mather, "Some Objections Against Imposition in Ordination," Richard Mather MS., American Antiquarian Society, Worcester, Mass. p. 2.

6. Nathaniel B. Shurtleff, ed., *The Records of the Governor and Company of the Massachusetts Bay* (Boston, 1853-55), I, 168. Hereafter referred to as *Records of Massachusetts Bay.*

7. The description given is a composite account from Mather's "A Plea for the Churches of Christ in New England," Part 3, 367, Massachusetts Historical Society, Boston, Mass.; Edward Johnson, *Wonder-Working Providence of Sions Savior in New England,* in *Original Narratives of Early American History,* ed. J. Franklin Jameson (New York, 1910), pp. 215-16; Winthrop, *Journal,* I, 173-74, 199, 292.

8. Winthrop, *Journal,* I, pp. 177-78.

9. Ibid.; Richard Mather, note included in letter of Thomas Shepard to Richard Mather, April 2, 1636, Cotton Mather MSS., Massachusetts Historical Society, Boston, Mass.

10. Richard Mather to Thomas Shepard, Cotton Mather MSS., Massachusetts Historical Society, Boston, Mass.

11. Increase Mather, *Life of Richard Mather,* p. 10; Richard Mather, note included in letter of Thomas Shepard to Richard Mather, April 2, 1636, Cotton Mather MSS., Massachusetts Historical Society, Boston, Mass.

12. Richard Mather, *A Catechisme or, The Grounds and Principles of Christian Religion* (London, 1650). Although the *Catechisme* was not written and published until many years after the rejection of the proposed Dorchester church, there was no change in the nonconformist explanation and justification of predestination in the years between 1636 and 1650. The arguments Mather used with his Dorchester congregants were undoubtedly the same he later wrote into his *Catechisme.*

13. Ibid., p. 17.

14. Increase Mather, *Life of Richard Mather,* p. 24.

15. Samuel J. Barrows and William B. Trask, eds., *Records of the First Church at Dorchester in New England, 1636-1734* (Boston, 1891), p. 2.

16. Richard Mather, "A Letter of Richard Mather to a Cleric in Old England," *William and Mary Quarterly* 3d ser., 29 (1972): 81-98. Questions 17 and 18 evidently were answered in an earlier letter and Mather did not repeat the answers he had already once given.

Chapter Three

1. Winthrop, *Journal,* I, 279.

2. The manuscript of "An Apologie for Church Covenant" is not extant.

All quotations are taken from the later published edition, *An Apologie of the Churches in New-England for Church Covenant* (London, 1643), p. 3.

3. J. Hammond Trumbull, ed., "Conference of the Elders of Massachusetts With the Reverend Robert Lenthal, of Weymouth," *Congregational Quarterly* 19 (1877): 239.

4. The manuscript of "An Answer to Two and Thirty Questions" is not extant. All quotations are taken from the later published edition, *Church Government and Church Covenant Discussed In an Answer of the Elders of the Several Churches in New-England to Two and Thirty Questions* (London, 1643).

5. Thomas J. Holmes, "Notes on Richard Mather's *Church Government,* London, 1643," *Proceedings of the American Antiquarian Society* 33 (1924): 239, 294.

6. *Keys to the Kingdom of Heaven* (London, 1644).

7. *The Independency on Scriptures of the Independency of Churches* (London, 1643).

8. Williston Walker, "The Services of the Mathers in New England Religious Development," *Papers of the American Society of Church History* 5 (1893): 65.

9. *A Modest and Brotherly Answer to Mr. Charles Herle* (London, 1644).

10. *A Survey of the Summe of Church Discipline* (London, 1648).

11. W[illiam] R[athband], *A Brief Narration of Some Church Courses . . . in New England* (London, 1644).

12. Thomas Weld[e], *An Answer to W.R.* (London, 1644).

13. Richard Mather, *An Heart-Melting Exhortation* (London, 1650), author's note at end of volume.

Chapter Four

1. Zoltan Haraszti, *The Enigma of the Bay Psalm Book* (Chicago, 1956), pp. 8-9.

2. Winthrop, *Journal,* I, viii; *An Account of the Bay Psalm Book,* in *Papers of the Hymn Society of America,* No. 7 (New York: The Hymn Society of America, 1940), p. 6.

3. Harold S. Jantz, "The First Century of New England Verse," *Proceedings of the American Antiquarian Society* 53 (1943): 237.

4. *Records of Massachusetts Bay,* II, 71.

5. The printing of election sermons did not become customary until approximately twenty years later. George P. Winship, *The Cambridge Press 1638-1692* (Philadelphia, 1945), p. 48.

6. William Perkins, *Works* (Cambridge, Eng., 1609), II, 736-37.

7. Richard Mather, "The Summe of Seventie Lectures on the First Chapter of the Second Epistle of Peter," Richard Mather MS., American Antiquarian Society, Worcester, Mass; Thomas Lechford, *Plain Dealing or News from New-England* (London, 1642), pp. 16-17, 19; John Cotton, *The Way of the Churches of Christ in New England* (London, 1645), p. 67; *Records of Massachusetts Bay*, III, 109-10; Winthrop, *Journal*, I, 324-26; Richard Mather's sermon notes are held by the American Antiquarian Society, Worcester, Mass.

8. William Haller, *The Rise of Puritanism* (New York, 1957), pp. 19, 50-51, 70; Patrick Collinson, *The Elizabethan Puritan Movement* (London, 1967), pp. 39-40, 49, 184, 258; Max Weber, *The Sociology of Religion* (Boston: Beacon Press, 1963), p. 43.

9. David Korbin, "The Expansion of the Visible Church in New England: 1629–1650," *Church History* 36 (1967): 192-93; Darrett B. Rutman, *American Puritanism: Faith and Practice* (Philadelphia, 1970), p. 15.

10. Ziff, *John Cotton*, pp. 29-31, 41-42.

11. Richard Mather, "The Summe of Seventie Lectures," pp. 13-14.

Chapter Five

1. For a fuller discussion of the events relating to the trial and banishment of Williams, see Ziff, *John Cotton, passim;* Winthrop, *Journal,* I, 62.

2. *Records of Massachusetts Bay,* I, 160–61.

3. Ibid., p. 168.

4. Winthrop, *Journal,* I, 326–27, 331, II, 19–20, 22–23, 46–48; Cotton Mather, *Magnalia,* III, 53–54, 78; Massachusetts Archives (Ecclesiastical) X, 26–30, State House, Boston, Mass.; *Records of Massachusetts Bay,* I, 274–75; Edmund S. Morgan, *Roger Williams: The Church and the State* (New York, 1967), pp. 75–76; Morgan, ed., *Puritan Political Ideas, 1558–1794* (Indianapolis, Ind., 1965), p. xxv; Thomas Lechford, *Plain Dealing,* p. 14.

5. Johnson, *Wonder-Working Providence,* pp. 98–99; Walker, *Creeds and Platforms of Congregationalism* (Boston, 1960), pp. 137–38. Joshua Coffin, *A Sketch of the History of Newbury, Newburyport and West Newbury from 1635–1845* (Boston, 1845), pp. 44–54; Cotton Mather, *Magnalia,* III, 143–148; Winthrop, *Journal,* II, 138–39.

6. For a complete discussion of the difficulties and disagreements on eligibility for baptism, see Morgan, *Visible Saints: The History of a Puritan Idea* (Ithaca, N.Y., 1965), pp. 129–38.

7. For extensive discussions of the conflicts between the clergy, the General Court, and the houses of the Court itself, see Winthrop, *Journal*, I, 133, 303, II, 86–88, 229–44; Robert E. Wall, Jr., *Massachusetts Bay: The Crucial Decade, 1640–1650* (New Haven, 1972), pp. 35–39, 70, 105, 144, 192–94, chap. 2; David D. Hall, *The Faithful Shepherd: A History of the New England Ministry in the Seventeenth Century* (Chapel Hill, N.C., 1972), pp. 129, 150–51.

8. Richard Mather, *Church Government . . . an Answer to Two and Thirty Questions*, pp. 82–83.

9. Ibid., pp. 64–65.

10. Winthrop, *Journal*, II, 274; *Records of Massachusetts Bay*, II, 155–56.

11. The report of the first session of the synod was entitled *The Result of a Synod at Cambridge in New England, Anno. 1646* (n.p., 1654), p. 71. Extracts in Williston Walker, *Creeds and Platforms of Congregationalism* (Boston, 1960), pp. 189–193.

12. *Result of a Synod*, p. 72.

13. Ibid.; Cotton Mather, *Magnalia*, V, 21–22.

14. Richard Mather, *Church Government . . . an Answer to Two and Thirty Questions*, pp. 63–64; Walker, "Services of the Mathers," p. 67; Holmes, "Notes on Richard Mather's *Church Government*," p. 296. (See periodical literature in Bibliography). For a complete discussion of Cotton's contribution see Ziff, *John Cotton*, p. 225, and Everett H. Emerson, *John Cotton* (New York, 1965), pp. 78–79.

15. Richard Mather, "A Modell of Church-Government," Richard Mather MS., American Antiquarian Society, Worcester, Mass., Arts. IX, X; *A Platform of Church Discipline* (Cambridge, Mass. Bay, 1649), Art. IX.

16. Ralph Partridge, "On Church Government Written About the Time the Platform Was Under Consideration," Ms. in American Antiquarian Society, Worcester, Mass., p. 11. The title is not the author's, but was added later. The manuscript was originally untitled and unheaded, the first sentence of the text beginning at the top of the first page. See also *Result of a Synod at Cambridge*, p. 19.

17. Cotton, *Way of the Churches of Christ*, p. 40.

18. Ibid., p. 6.

19. Ibid., p. 19.

20. Cotton, *Keys to the Kingdom of Heaven*, pp. 154, 156–57.

21. Art XVII, sec. 1; "Modell of Church-Government," p. 88.

22. *Platform of Church Discipline*, Art. XVII, sec. 2.

23. *Records of Massachusetts Bay*, III, 177–78.

24. A set of fifteen objections to the *Platform* entitled "Exceptions to some things in the Synod at Cambridge 1649" in an unidentified hand is among the Cotton Papers, III, item 10, Prince Collection, Boston Public Library, Boston, Mass.; Richard Mather, "An Answer of the Elders to Reasons Doubted and Objections Against Sundry Passages in the Platforme of Discipline," Richard Mather MS., American Antiquarian Society, Worcester, Mass., *passim.*; *Records of Massachusetts Bay*, III, 235–36, 240; Cotton Mather, *Magnalia*, V, 39. See also Richard Mather's letter to John Cotton on this subject. Richard Mather MS., American Antiquarian Society, Worcester, Mass.

25. "An Answer of the Elders," p. 4.

26. *Platform of Church Discipline*, Art. II, secs. 3, 4.

27. "An Answer of the Elders," p. 5.

28. *Records of Massachusetts Bay*, III, 240, IV, 1, 57–58.

29. Ibid.

30. *Platform of Church Discipline*, Art. XVII.

31. Ibid., Art. XV, sec. 3.

32. Ibid., Art. XVI, sec. 3.

33. Examples of secular interference in minor ecclesiastical matters after 1650 can be found frequently. See Massachusetts Archives (Ecclesiastical), X, 31–35, 44–55a, 74–83, 85–89; *Records of Massachusetts Bay*, IV, 1, 42, 43, 170–71, 113, 117, 227–28, 236, 309–10, 351, 378, 390, 393.

Chapter Six

1. Winthrop, *Journal*, II, 67.

2. Entitled *A Treatise Concerning the Lawful Subject of Baptism* (n.p., 1643).

3. Richard Mather, "An Answer to 9 Reasons of John Spilsbury to Prove Infants Ought Not to Be Baptized," American Antiquarian Society, Worcester, Mass., pp. 1, 4–5, 11–66.

4. Richard Mather, *Church Government . . . an Answer to Two and Thirty Questions*, p. 22.

5. Richard Mather, "Plea for the Churches of Christ in New England," Massachusetts Historical Society, Boston, Mass., Part 3, 232–33; Part 4, 47–48, 90.

6. Ibid., p. 71.

7. Ibid. Writing several years after his father's death, Increase Mather used quoted material from "Plea" to establish his father as a supporter of the half-way covenant as early as 1645. Unfortunately, the son used a passage taken from context that substantiated his contention, but did not see fit to

include the elder Mather's remarks showing his indecision on the subject. See Increase Mather, *First Principles of New England Concerning the Subject of Baptisme* (Cambridge, Mass. Bay, 1675), pp. 8–9.

8. Increase Mather, *First Principles*, pp. 5, 8–9, 13, 22, 23–24, 38.

9. *Fourth Report of the Record Commissioners of the City of Boston 1880, Dorchester Town Records*, 2d ed. (Boston, 1883), p. 63 *et passim*; Richard Mather, "Will," *New England Historical and Genealogical Register* 20 (1886):248–55.

10. Richard Mather, *An Answer to Two Questions* (Boston, 1712), pp. vii–viii.

11. Richard Mather, "The Summe of Seventie Lectures," p. 24.

12. Richard Mather, *An Answer to Two Questions*, pp. 9–10.

13. Increase Mather, *First Principles*, p. 11; *Records of the First Church at Dorchester*, pp. 164–65.

14. *Records of Massachusetts Bay*, III, 419, IV, 2, 280.

15. Richard Mather, *A Disputation Concerning Church-Members and Their Children In Answer to XXI Questions* (London, 1659), p. 1. All quotations are from the London edition. The 1657 manuscript referred to in the text is among the Richard Mather MSS., at American Antiquarian Society, Worcester, Mass.

16. *Records of the First Church at Dorchester*, p. 168.

17. Ibid., pp. 22, 33–34.

18. Hanna Minot was the daughter of the late Israel Stoughton, once one of Dorchester's leading citizens. James Minot was a son of George Minot, a founder of the church and a more important resident of the town. Lemuel Shattuck, "The Minott Family," *New England Historical and Genealogical Register*, I (1847), 171–72; *Records of the First Church at Dorchester*, pp. 33–36.

19. *Records of the First Church at Dorchester*, pp. 33–36.

20. Ibid., pp. 39–40.

21. Increase Mather, "Letter to John Davenport," October, 1662, reprinted in *Collections of the Massachusetts Historical Society*, 4th ser., 8 (1868): 205; *Records of the First Church at Dorchester*, p. 39; Jonathan Mitchel, *An Answer to the Apologetical Preface Published in the Name and Behalf of the Brethren that Dissented in the Late Synod* (Cambridge, Mass. Bay, 1664); John Davenport, *Another Essay for the Investigation of the Truth* (Cambridge, Mass. Bay, 1663), preface.

22. Charles Chauncy, *Anti-Synodalia Scripta Americana* (London, 1662); John Allin, *Animadversions Upon the Antisynodalia Americana* (Boston, 1664); Jonathan Mitchel's *Answer to the Apologetical Preface* was published

as a preface to Mather's tract supporting the determinations of the synod. The two works appeared under the single title, *A Defense of the Answer and Arguments of the Synod Met at Boston in the Year 1662* (Cambridge, Mass. Bay, 1664).

23. Increase Mather, *First Principles,* postscript, p. 7.

24. John Davenport, *Another Essay,* pp. 2, 4.

25. Cotton Mather, *Magnalia,* III, 47; Increase Mather, *Life of Richard Mather,* pp. 25–26; *Records of the First Church at Dorchester,* p. 55.

26. *Records of the First Church at Dorchester,* p. 55.

27. Cotton Mather, *Magnalia,* III, 38.

28. Isabel M. Calder, *Letters of John Davenport, Puritan Divine* (New Haven, 1937), pp. 10–11; Richard D. Pierce, ed., *Records of the First Church in Boston 1630–1868* in *Publications of the Colonial Society of Massachusetts* (Boston, 1961), XXIX, liii, 62.

29. Calder, *Letters of John Davenport,* p. 11; *Records of the First Church at Dorchester,* pp. 54–55; *Records of the First Church in Boston,* XXIX, liii, 62.

30. Calder, *Letters of John Davenport,* p. 11; *Records of the First Church at Dorchester,* p. 55; Cotton Mather, *Magnalia,* III, 129; Increase Mather, *Life of Richard Mather,* p. 26.

31. Increase Mather, *Life of Richard Mather,* pp. 25–29; Cotton Mather, *Magnalia,* III, 128, 129.

32. *Magnalia,* III, p. 129.

Chapter Seven

1. Jonathan Mitchel, *Nehemiah on the Wall in Troublesome Times* (Cambridge, Mass. Bay, 1670), pp. 6–7, 16, 28, 31–32.

2. William Stoughton, *New Englands True Interest* (Cambridge, Mass. Bay, 1670), p. 13.

3. John Davenport, *A Sermon Preach'd at the Election of the Governor, at Boston in New England* (Cambridge, Mass. Bay, 1670), pp. 6, 12, 13.

4. *Records of Massachusetts Bay,* IV:2, 490.

5. Hall, *Faithful Shepherd,* pp. 235–37.

6. Thomas Shepard, Jr., *Eye-Salve, Or A Watchword from Our Lord Jesus Christ unto His Church* (Cambridge, Mass. Bay, 1673), p. 13.

7. Urian Oakes, *New England Pleaded With* (Cambridge, Mass. Bay, 1673), pp. 25–26, 54–55.

Selected Bibliography

PRIMARY SOURCES

Almost every account of the life and work of Richard Mather contains at least some bibliographical data, but the only record of his manuscripts and published works that approaches completeness is that compiled by Thomas J. Holmes in *The Minor Mathers, A List of their Works* (Cambridge, Mass.: Harvard University Press, 1940).

1. Manuscript Collections
The largest and most valuable collection of Richard Mather's surviving manuscripts is held at the American Antiquarian Society, Worcester, Massachusetts. Included with the material are Ralph Partridge's "On Church Government" and Jonathan Mitchel's draft preface to Mather's *Defense of the Answer and Arguments of the Synod Met at Boston In the Year 1662.* The collection also contains copies made by Mather of letters written by other clerics, several minor items, a number of manuscript fragments, and half a dozen pieces of uncertain authorship. The major pieces by Richard Mather at the American Antiquarian Society are:
"An Answer of the Elders to Certayne Doubts and Objections Against Sundry Passages in the Platforme of Discipline."
"Answer to 9 Reasons of John Spilsbury to Prove that Infants Ought Not to Be Baptized."
"An Answer to the Twenty-One Questions Submitted by the General Court at Hartford to the General Court at Boston."
"Modell of Church-Government."
"Observations and Arguments Respecting the Government of Christian Churches."
"Platform of Church Discipline."
"Some Objections Against Imposition in Ordination."
"The Summe of Seventie Lectures Upon the First Chapter of the Second Epistle of Peter."
"Whether the Power of Church Government Bee in All the People or in the Elders Alone."

The Boston Public Library holds several letters of Richard Mather, a list of books he borrowed in 1647, and a short tract entitled "The Singing of Psalms." The letters and the book list were printed in the *Collections of the Massachusetts Historical Society,* 4th ser., 8 (1868): 69-77.

The Henry E. Huntington Library and Art Gallery, San Marino, California, holds the manuscript of *An Heart-Melting Exhortation* and another fragment from an unidentified work.

Richard Mather's "Plea for the Churches of Christ in New England" and the brief exchange of notes between Mather and Thomas Shepard in April, 1636, are held by the Massachusetts Historical Society, Boston, Mass. A 1636 letter by Mather to an unidentified English cleric, the text of which is contained in "Plea," has been published in the *William and Mary Quarterly* 29 (1972): 81-98.

John Minot's book of notes taken on Richard Mather's sermons, a manuscript copy of *Church Government . . . an Answer to Two and Thirty Questions* (possibly in the hand of John Cotton), several sermons, sermon fragments, and a facsimile letter are in the collection of Mather material at the University of Virginia at Charlottesville.

Assorted minor manuscripts, handwritten copies of letters and other items, manuscript fragments, and sermons are held by The Historical Society of Chicago, The New York Public Library, Yale University, and The Historical Society of Pennsylvania.

2. Published Works by Richard Mather

An Answer to Two Questions: Whether Does the Power of Church Government Belong to all the People or to the Elders Alone. Boston, 1712.

An Apologie of The Churches in New England for Church Covenant. London, 1643.

A Catechisme or, The Grounds and Principles of Christian Religion. London, 1650.

Church Government and Church Covenant Discussed, In an Answer of the Elders of the Several Churches in New-England to Two and Thirty Questions. London, 1643.

A Defense of the Answer and Arguments of the Synod met at Boston in the year 1662. Cambridge, Mass. Bay, 1664.

A Disputation Concerning Church-Members and Their Children in Answer to XXI Questions. London, 1659.

A Farewel-Exhortation to the Church and People of Dorchester in New England. Cambridge, Mass. Bay, 1657.

An Heart-Melting Exhortation, Together with a Cordiall Consolation, Presented in a Letter from New-England, to Their Dear Countrymen of Lancashire. London, 1650. (With William Tompson)

Journal. Published in the *Collections of the Dorchester Antiquarian and Historical Society,* No. 3. Boston: David Clapp, 1850.

A Modest and Brotherly Answer to Mr. Charles Herle his Book, Against the Independency of Churches. London, 1644. (With William Tompson)

A Platform of Church Discipline Gathered out of the Word of God. Cambridge, Mass. Bay, 1649.

A Reply to Mr. Rutherford, or, A Defence of the Answer to Reverend Mr. Herles Booke Against the Independency of Churches. London, 1646.

The Summe of Certain Sermons upon Genes: 15. 6. Cambridge, Mass. Bay, 1652.

"To the Christian Reader." Preface in John Eliot and Thomas Mayhew's *Tears of Repentence: or, A Further Narrative of the Progress of the Gospel Amongst the Indians in New England.* London, 1653.

"Will." Printed in full in the *New England Historical and Genealogical Register* 20 (1866): 248-55.

3. Records and Journals

Barrows, Samuel J. and Trask, William B., eds. *Records of the First Church at Dorchester in New England, 1636-1734.* Boston: George H. Ellis, 1891.

Lowenberg, W.J., ed. *The Registers of the Parish Church of Bury in the County of Lancaster.* Rochdale, Eng.: Lancashire Parish Register Society, 1898.

Picton, J.K., ed. *Selections from the Municipal Archives and Records of Liverpool from the 13th to the 17th Century Inclusive.* 2 vols. Liverpool: Gilbert G. Walmsey, 1883.

Pierce, Richard D., ed. *Records of the First Church in Boston 1630-1868.* In *Publications of the Colonial Society of Massachusetts,* Vols. 29, 30, 31. Boston: Colonial Society of Massachusetts, 1961.

Report of the Record Commissioners of the City of Boston 1800: Dorchester Town Records. Boston: Rockwell and Churchill, 1883.

Shurtleff, Nathaniel B., ed. *Records of the Governor and Company of the Massachusetts Bay.* 5 vols. Boston: William White, 1853-55.

Smith, Arthur, ed. *Registers of the Parish Church of Walton-on-the-Hill.* Wigan, Eng.: Lancashire Parish Register Society, 1900.

Sparke, Archibald, ed. *Parish Registers of Warrington 1591-1653.* Preston, Eng.: Lancashire Parish Register Society, 1933.

Winthrop, John. *Journal History of New England.* Edited by J. K. Hosmer. 2 vols. In *Original Narratives of Early American History.* New York: Charles Scribner's Sons, 1908.

SECONDARY SOURCES

1. Works on Mather's Life and Writings
   In addition to innumerable accounts contained in footnotes, there are a quantity of abbreviated studies of Richard Mather and one book-length biography.
BEAMONT, WILLIAM. *Winwick: Its History and Antiquities.* Warrington, Eng.: Guardian Steam Printing Works, 1875. A brief account of Mather's life, salted with inaccuracies, is included with the history of Winwick.
BROOK, BENJAMIN. *The Lives of the Puritans.* London: James Black, 1813. Most of Brook's information is from works by Samuel Clarke, Anthony à Wood, and Cotton Mather.
BURG, B.R. *Richard Mather of Dorchester.* Lexington, Ky.: University Press of Kentucky, 1976. The only scholarly, comprehensive biography of Richard Mather available.
CLARKE, SAMUEL. *The Lives of Sundry Eminent Persons in this Later Age.* London: 1683. Despite the fact that Clarke actually knew Mather, there is nothing from the acquaintance that is included in the work.
DAVIS, VALENTINE D. *Some Account of the Ancient Chapel of Toxteth Park Liverpool.* Liverpool: Henry Young, 1884. The book contains a brief account of Mather's life and work.
MATHER, COTTON. *Magnalia Christi Americana.* London: 1702. A short sketch of Richard Mather's life is included along with scores of clerical biographies in the *Magnalia.* It is based almost entirely on the earlier biography by Increase Mather.
MATHER, HORACE E. *The Lineage of Rev. Richard Mather.* Hartford: Case, Lockwood and Brainard, 1890. A genealogical work that adds a few biographical details to the information already available on Richard Mather.
MATHER, INCREASE. *The Life and Death of That Reverend Man of God, Mr. Richard Mather.* Cambridge, Mass. Bay, 1670. The book is the labor of an adoring son and must be read with that in mind. Since it is the basic source for all studies of Richard Mather, it is used as the only reference in many citations in the present work although the same event may be described in several other secondary sources. Increase Mather's biography

of his father has been reprinted in the *Collections of the Dorchester Antiquarian and Historical Society*, No. 3 (Boston: David Clapp, Jr., 1850). A facsimile reprint edited by William K. Bottorff and Benjamin Franklin V is also available from the Department of English, University of Ohio, Athens, Ohio.

WALKER, WILLISTON. *Ten New England Leaders*. New York: Silver, Burdett, 1901. One of the few short biographies of Richard Mather that contain perceptive commentary on his work.

WOOD, ANTHONY à. *Athenae Oxoniensis*. 3d ed. London: F.C. and J. Rivington, 1817. Mather is included in Wood's work by virtue of his attendance at Oxford.

2. Works written before 1800

ALLIN, JOHN. *Animadversions Upon the Antisynodalia Americana*. Boston, 1664. Allin's work is essential to an understanding of the issues as they were defined by the participants in the controversy that followed the synod of 1662.

Bay Psalm Book. See *The Whole Book of Psalms*.

CHAUNCY, CHARLES. *Anti-Synodalia Scripta Americana*. [London], 1662. Like John Allin's *Animadversions,* Chauncy's rebuttal to the majority party in the synod of 1662 is essential to any understanding of the disagreement over the administration of baptism.

COTTON, JOHN. *The Keys to the Kingdom of Heaven and Power Thereof*. London, 1644, Cotton's definitive treatise on the divine justification for the congregational churches in New England.

————. *The Way of the Churches of Christ in New England*. London, 1645. Although published after *Keys to the Kingdom of Heaven*, this was Cotton's first spiritual justification of congregational polity, and though it was never repudiated by its author, neither did he consider it as authoritative as the *Keys*. Both works owe a considerable debt to Richard Mather's early defenses of Bay Colony religious practice, but they differ in that while Mather attempted to justify local procedures on a pragmatic basis, by the time Cotton wrote, the need was to justify them as the will of God.

————. *The Way of the Congregational Churches Cleared*. London, 1648. Like Mather, Cotton was also called upon to defend Massachusetts Bay from presbyterian attacks. In *The Way of the Congregational Churches,* Cotton defends congregationalism against charges of separatism, discusses the nature of the colony's religion, and gives his own account of the Antinomian controversy of 1637. The book is also a plea for harmony between congregationalist and presbyterian.

DAVENPORT, JOHN. *Another Essay for the Investigation of the Truth.* Cambridge, Mass. Bay, 1663. The most powerful attack against extending eligibility for baptism by the foremost opponent of the majority party in the synod of 1662.

————. *An Answer of the Elders of the Several Churches in New England unto 9 Propositions.* London, 1643. Printed and bound with Mather's two defenses of Bay Colony practice in the attempt to influence the course of religious development in England.

HERLE, CHARLES. *The Independency on Scriptures of the Independency of Churches.* London, 1643. One of the earliest published challenges to congregational polity from a presbyterian.

HOOKER, THOMAS. *A Survey of the Summe of Church Discipline.* London, 1648. The colonial answer to Samuel Rutherford's presbyterian attacks.

JOHNSON, EDWARD. *Wonder-Working Providence of Sions Savior in New England.* Edited by J. Franklin Jameson. In *Original Narratives of Early American History.* New York: Charles Scribner's Sons, 1910. A firsthand account of many of the struggles in the Bay Colony's initial decade by an ardent partisan.

LECHFORD, THOMAS. *Plain Dealing or News from New England.* London, 1642. An early attack on New England.

MATHER, COTTON. *Magnalia Christi Americana: Or the Ecclesiastical History of New England.* London, 1702. An all-encompassing account of the glories of New England's first eighty years of settlement by one of the Bay Colony's most articulate leaders.

MATHER, INCREASE. *The First Principles of New England Concerning the Subject of Baptisme and Communion of Churches.* Cambridge, Mass. Bay, 1675. A defense of the half-way covenant written after Increase had changed from an opponent to a champion of broadened eligibility for baptism. It is the only account of Richard Mather's earliest efforts to persuade his clerical associates of the divine sanction for widening eligibility for baptism.

MITCHEL, JONATHAN. *An Answer to the Apologetical Preface.* Cambridge, Mass. Bay, 1664. The synodalian reply to Increase Mather's preface to Davenport's attack on the half-way covenant.

PERKINS, WILLIAM. *Works.* 3 vols. Cambridge, Eng., 1609. A guide to all aspects of English nonconformity that was widely used by most dissenting clerics.

R[ATHBAND], W[ILLIAM]. *A Brief Narration of Some Church Courses Held in Opinion and Practice in the Churches Lately Erected in New*

England. London, 1644. A scurrilous attack on Richard Mather's defenses of Bay Colony church practice.

RUTHERFORD, SAMUEL. *The Due Right of Presbyteries.* London, 1644. An attack on New England church polity by a leading Scottish divine.

SPILSBURY, JOHN. *A Treatise Concerning the Lawful Subject of Baptism.* n.p., 1643. A series of arguments against the type of paedobaptism practiced by most English clerics in the homeland and in America. It was answered by Richard Mather.

WELD[E], THOMAS, *An Answer to W.R.* [William Rathband]. London, 1644. The first New England reply to Rathband's presbyterian criticisms of the colony's religion.

The Whole Book of Psalms Faithfully Translated in English Metre. Cambridge, Mass. Bay, 1640. First book printed in English North America. Several of the psalms were translated from the Hebrew by Mather.

3. Monographs and Special Studies Written since 1800

BATTIS, EMERY. *Saints and Sectaries: Anne Hutchinson and the Antinomian Controversy in the Massachusetts Bay Colony.* Chapel Hill, N.C.: University of North Carolina Press for the Institute of Early American History and Culture at Williamsburg, Virginia, 1962. An early attempt by an American historian to use quantitative data to interpret one phase of the Massachusetts Bay Colony's past.

CALDER, ISABEL M., ed. *Letters of John Davenport, Puritan Divine.* New Haven, Yale University Press, 1937. Well-edited collection with valuable introductory comments.

COFFIN, JOSHUA. *A Sketch of the History of Newbury, Newburyport, and West Newbury from 1635–1845.* Boston: Samuel G. Drake, 1845. Lengthy local history containing considerable factual material.

COLLINSON, PATRICK. *The Elizabethan Puritan Movement.* London: Jonathan Cape, 1967. One of the more useful works on religious dissent in sixteenth-century England.

COMMITTEE OF THE DORCHESTER ANTIQUARIAN SOCIETY. *History of the Town of Dorchester Massachusetts.* Boston: n.p., 1859. The best of several inadequate histories of Dorchester available.

DEXTER, HENRY M. *The Congregationalism of the Last Three Hundred Years, As Seen in its Literature.* New York: Harper Brothers, 1880. A heavily detailed antiquarian work most valuable for its extensive bibliographical appendix.

EMERSON, EVERETT H. *John Cotton.* New York: Twayne, 1965.

Contains an excellent discussion of Cotton's influence on the composition of the *Cambridge Platform.*

HALL, DAVID D. *The Faithful Shepherd: A History of the New England Ministry in the Seventeenth Century.* Chapel Hill, N.C.: University of North Carolina Press for the Institute of Early American History and Culture, Williamsburg, Virginia, 1972. A valuable study of the first two generations of New England clergy and their attempt to define their role in America.

HALLER, WILLIAM. *The Rise of Puritanism.* Torchbook ed. New York: Harper and Row, 1957. A very perceptive study of the origin and early history of English nonconformity.

HARASZTI, ZOLTAN. *The Enigma of the Bay Psalm Book.* Chicago: University of Chicago Press, 1956. An impressive piece of research that revises several centuries of scholarship on the *Bay Psalm Book.*

LEVY, BABETTE M. *Preaching in the First Half Century of New England History.* In *Studies in Church History,* Vol. 4. Matthew Spinka and Robert H. Nichols, eds. Hartford: American Society of Church History, 1945.

MIDDLEKAUFF, ROBERT. *The Mathers: Three Generations of Puritan Intellectuals, 1596–1728.* New York: Oxford University Press, 1971. In his work with Richard Mather's sermons, Middlekauff has asked questions very different from my own, and the result is two presentations that are divergent in thrust and direction. This is not an assertion of the existence of two contending interpretations. We have examined the same material from different perspectives and our observations are understandably different.

MILLER, PERRY. *Errand into the Wilderness.* Torchbook ed. New York: Harper and Row, 1964. It is customary in any work on early New England to acknowledge a debt to Perry Miller, for without his articles and books it is difficult to imagine what direction colonial American studies might have taken.

―――. *The New England Mind from Colony to Province.* Cambridge, Mass.: Harvard University Press, 1952. Miller's landmark study of New England intellectual evolution.

―――. *The New England Mind: The 17th Century.* Cambridge, Mass., Harvard University Press, 1939. By far the most brilliant and far-ranging interpretation of the intellectual history of early America.

―――. *Orthodoxy in Massachusetts.* Cambridge, Mass.: Harvard University Press, 1933. Exploration of the background and substance of Massachusetts Bay's earliest religious thought.

MITCHELL, W. FRASER. *English Pulpit Oratory from Andrewes to*

Tillotson: A Study of its Literary Aspects. London: Society for Promoting
Christian Knowledge, 1932. A fine study of the type of pulpit oratory
nonconformists reacted against in the age of Elizabeth and the early
Stuarts.

MORGAN, EDMUND S., ed. *Puritan Political Ideas, 1558-1794,* Indianapolis, Ind.: Bobbs-Merrill Co., 1965. Morgan's introduction is especially
helpful in understanding the relationship between church and state in the
Massachusetts Bay Colony.

———. *Visible Saints: The History of a Puritan Idea.* Ithaca, N.Y.:
Cornell University Press, 1965. The best interpretation available of the
controversy over eligibility for baptism.

MURDOCK, KENNETH B. *Increase Mather: The Foremost American
Puritan.* Cambridge, Mass.: Harvard University Press, 1925. Exceedingly
favorable treatment of Increase Mather, but still a valuable biography of
Richard Mather's youngest and most brilliant son.

NIGHTINGALE, BENJAMIN. *Lancashire Nonconformity; or Sketches
Historical and Descriptive of the Congregational and Old Presbyterian
Churches in the County.* 3 vols. Manchester: John Heywood, 1891.
Contains considerable information on individual churches in the area
dating back to the sixteenth century.

PARRY, MILMAN. "A Comparative Study of Diction As One of the
Elements of Style in Early Greek Poetry." Master of Arts Thesis.
University of California, Berkeley, 1922. Some methodological direction
for analyzing Mather's sermons was provided by this landmark study of
oral interpretation.

POPE, ROBERT G. *The Half-Way Covenant, Church Membership in
Puritan New England.* Princeton, N.J.: Princeton University Press, 1969.
Monographic study of the division between church factions over eligibility
for baptism in both the Massachusetts Bay Colony and in Connecticut.
Pope argues the dispute was a confrontation over polity rather than over
baptism.

RUTMAN, DARRETT B. *American Puritanism: Faith and Practice.*
Philadelphia: Lippincott, 1970. Although severely criticized, the work is a
daring, if not entirely successful, attempt to lay the foundation for a new
interpretive synthesis of early New England's past.

WALKER, WILLISTON. *The Creeds and Platforms of Congregationalism.*
1893. Reprint. Boston: Pilgrim Press, 1960. A detailed account of many
of the religious disputes that plagued New England. The work is especially
valuable not only for the quality of the investigation but for the reprints of
many vital documents that it contains.

WALL, ROBERT E. *Massachusetts Bay: The Crucial Decade, 1640–1650.* New Haven: Yale University Press, 1972. Particularly useful for its discussion of the split between the deputies and the assistants in the General Court.

WALZER, MICHAEL. *The Revolution of the Saints: A Study in the Origins of Radical Politics.* Cambridge, Mass.: Harvard University Press, 1965. An invaluable study that gives an awareness of the techniques of organization as well as a feeling for the revolutionary intensity of English nonconformity during the reigns of Elizabeth, James I, and Charles I.

WINSHIP, GEORGE P. *The Cambridge Press 1638–1692.* Philadelphia: University of Pennsylvania Press, 1945. Some information on the *Bay Psalm Book* unavailable elsewhere.

YOUNG, ALEXANDER. *Chronicles of the First Planters of the Colony of Massachusetts Bay, From 1623 to 1636.* 1846. Reprint, New York: Da Capo Press, 1970. Finest available collection of the earliest surviving Bay Colony documents. Includes the journal of Richard Mather written on the ocean crossing in 1635.

ZIFF, LARZER. *The Career of John Cotton: Puritanism and the American Experience.* Princeton, N.J.: Princeton University Press, 1962. Careful examination and evaluation of the labors of Cotton.

4. Periodical Literature and Organizational Publications

BRIDGEMAN, GEORGE T.O. *The History of the Church and Manor at Wigan in the County of Lancaster. From Remains Historical and Literary Connected with the Palatine Counties of Lancashire and Chester.* Vol. 16, Part 2. Manchester: The Cheltenham Society, 1889. Some factual information about the area where Mather spent his youth and about the grammar school he attended.

BLAKE, JAMES. *Annals of the Town of Dorchester.* In *Collections of the Dorchester Antiquarian and Historical Society,* No. 2. Boston: David Clapp, Jr., 1846. Brief account of the town's history with particular emphasis on the early years.

FOXE, JOHN. *The Acts and Monuments of the Christian Religion.* 1563. Reprint. New York: AMS Press, 1965. Next to the Bible, the most widely read popular religious work in England and New England during the seventeenth century.

HALL, LAWRENCE. "The Ancient Chapel of Toxteth Park and Toxteth School." *Historic Society of Lancashire and Cheshire,* 87 (1936): 23-57. The article is an antiquarian account of the church and school where

Mather taught and preached before coming to America.

———— "Toxteth Park Chapel in the 17th Century." *Transactions of the Unitarian Historical Society,* 5 (1934): 351-83. Similar to Hall's article published by the Historic Society of Lancashire and Cheshire in 1936, it provides additional information on Mather's first church.

HOLMES, THOMAS J. "Notes on Richard Mather's *Church Government,* London, 1643." *Proceedings of the American Antiquarian Society,* 33 (1924): 291-96. The article provides bibliographical data on one of Mather's most important works.

JANTZ, HAROLD S. "The First Century of New England Verse." *Proceedings of the American Antiquarian Society,* 53, Part 2 (1943): 219-508. Some discussion of Mather's lack of poetic skill as evidenced by his translations in the *Bay Psalm Book.*

KORBIN, DAVID. "The Expansion of the Visible Church in New England: 1629–1650." *Church History* 36 (1967): 189-200. Interpretive account of attempts by early New England church members to restructure the theology of church membership to accommodate evangelism.

MILLER, PERRY. "The Half Way Covenant." *New England Quarterly* 6 (1933): 676-715. A dated but still extremely valuable interpretation of the conflict over extending eligibility for baptism.

MURDOCK, KENNETH B. "Richard Mather." *Old Time New England,* 15 (1924): 51-57. Brief survey of factual material available on Mather.

SHATTUCK, LEMUEL. "The Minott Family." *New England Historical and Genealogical Register,* 1 (1847): 171-78. Careful account of one of Dorchester's most important families.

SIMMONS, RICHARD. "The Founding of the Third Church in Boston." *William and Mary Quarterly* 26 (1969): 241-52. One of the best interpretive studies of the schism in the First Church in Boston and the subsequent gathering of the Third Church.

SWIFT, LINDSAY. "Massachusetts Election Sermons." *Publications of the Colonial Society of Massachusetts* 1 (1894): 388-451. An extended piece on the origins, direction, and impact of the annual election sermon on the politics and religious life of the Massachusetts Bay Colony.

TRUMBULL, J. HAMMOND. ed. "Conference of the Elders of Massachusetts With the Reverend Robert Lenthal, of Weymouth, Held at Dorchester, Feb. 10, 1639." *Congregational Quarterly* 19 (1877): 239. Partial account, including transcription of testimony, giving an excellent idea of the manner in which Bay Colony clerics moved to correct an erring colleague.

WALKER, WILLISTON. "The Services of the Mathers in New England Religious Development." *Papers of the American Society of Church History* V (1893): 59-85. Some analysis of Richard Mather's contribution to the establishment of the religious settlement in the Bay.

Index